The M
PEARLER'S
DAUGHTER

Rosemary Hemphill was born in 1922 in Broome, on Australia's north-west coast. Her childhood was divided between Broome and her grandparents' home in Bromley, England, where her love of gardens and herbs and all things green and scented was born.

Together with her husband, John, Rosemary established Australia's first herb-growing business, Somerset Cottage, at Dural, north of Sydney, after the Second World War. For over forty years, Rosemary and John were involved in the cultivation, drying, blending and retailing of herbs, many of which were largely unknown in Australia at that time. Their work helped, and continues to help, Australians to use a wide variety of herbs in their cooking. Rosemary and John wrote numerous books both together and separately. Rosemary now lives in Sydney.

ALSO BY ROSEMARY HEMPHILL
Fragrance and Flavour
Spice and Savour
A Gift Book of Herbs and Flowers
Herbs for All Seasons

For children
Look, You Can Cook
Cooking is Fun

TOGETHER WITH JOHN HEMPHILL
Herbs and Spices
Herbs: Their Cultivation and Use
Herbs for Health
What Herb Is That?
Myths and Legends of the Garden

The MASTER PEARLER'S DAUGHTER

ROSEMARY HEMPHILL

PAN

Pan Macmillan Australia

First published 2004 in Macmillan by Pan Macmillan Australia Pty Limited
This edition published 2005 in Pan by Pan Macmillan Australia Pty Limited
St Martins Tower, 31 Market Street, Sydney

National Library of Australia
cataloguing-in-publication data:

Hemphill, Rosemary.
The master pearler's daughter: memories of my Broome childhood.

ISBN 0 330 42203 0.

1. Hemphill, Rosemary – Childhood and youth.
2. Broome (W.A.) – Social life and customs. I. Title

994.14042092

Typeset in 11.5/14.5 Bembo by Post Pre-press Group
Printed in Australia by McPherson's Printing Group
Cover and internal design by Nada Backovic
Cover photograph by Joe Filshie
Internal photographs from the author's family albums
Frangipani photographs by Benedict Foley

Photograph on page x: A Blue Funnel 'school ship'.
Photograph on page 64: Mother and me, aged four, in Perth in 1926.
Photograph on page 134: New Farm's drawing room opened onto a glass-roofed,
wisteria-hung terrace.
Photograph on page 192: Margery Stanton and me at seventeen, doing the swing in our
back garden in Broome in 1939.
Photograph on page 248: A natural pearl.

*To my late English maternal grandparents, Frederick
and Catherine Sprang, with loving thanks for my years at New
Farm, and for their example and generosity, which shaped my life.*

*And to my late parents, Louis and Doris Goldie,
who were among the brave pearling pioneers of Broome.*

Contents

Part I

Broome, December 1936

On a hot sunny morning in early December 1936 there is a clamorous hubbub of noise and activity on Fremantle's Number 3 wharf. MV *Gorgon*, Blue Funnel Line's sparkling new ship, will soon be casting off for the open sea. The jangled mix of sounds comes from machinery loading cargo into its hold; men shouting and whistling; trucks and cars coming and going; squeals of laughter from teenage girls; hoarse bursts of 'Oi', the favourite greeting of the moment, from boys. We are beginning to board the ship for the annual pre-Christmas voyage along the desolate north-west coast of Western Australia and on into Asian waters.

The vessel is carrying Australian schoolchildren to Geraldton, Carnarvon, Cossack, Port Hedland and Broome. Nearly all the Broome group come from pearling families and our homes are on the coast; a few of the others who leave the ship with us live on faraway cattle stations in the Kimberley. The trip from Fremantle to Broome takes nearly a week.

From Broome and the Indian Ocean, *Gorgon* sails through the Timor and Java Seas to Surabaya and Batavia, where the Dutch passengers disembark. Finally she crosses the Strait of Malacca to Singapore and, voyage completed, the last students go ashore, home to their English parents. In several days, after taking on more cargo and passengers, *Gorgon* will turn around and follow the same route in reverse. At the end of January we will sail back to Perth and boarding school.

The 'school ship' is avoided by adults, who prefer to take the trip at an earlier or later time: scores of rowdy youngsters are not ideal fellow travellers. The boys are especially unruly, running all over the ship, climbing over the rails for dares, racing up and down companionways, making a terrific din.

There is the true story, the boys gleefully tell us, of a recent school ship returning to Hong Kong and Singapore from England, which was boarded by Chinese pirates in the South China Seas: all they got was pocket money, chewing gum, marbles, penknives, Minties, and an incredible lot of cheek. The outlaws gave up in disgust and gladly left the steamer to continue on its way.

On the wharf, cranes are finishing loading cargo, and now passengers' trunks are being winched on board. Excitement mounts. We are starting our eight-week Christmas holidays and we are jubilant. Four of us in blue and grey St Hilda's uniforms have been driven to the quay by a boarding school mistress: Lieke, Cynthia, Mollie and me. She tells us to have a happy Christmas, be good girls, and she waves goodbye. We are in our early teens and our hormones are beginning to surge.

I'm glad Mollie is coming to stay for Christmas; she's good company, a little older than me, and taller. We both part our hair in the middle and plait it into long pigtails. Mollie has golden lights in her brown hair, her heart-shaped face is framed with soft curls, her eyes are dark blue, there's a dimple in her chin; the boys like her, she has sex appeal. My hair is reddish-brown. I'm small for a fourteen-year-old, have hazel eyes, freckles and adolescent plumpness.

Seeing friends, we call in shrill animated voices to Pam, Peggy and Suzanne in their Perth College navy and white uniforms. They are walking to the gangway, carrying small suitcases. We run quickly over to them, clutching our cases too. Our trunks are going straight to our cabins.

Lieke is breathless with anticipation. 'How cracker! Over a week on ze ship, to Batavia and home until ze end of January! Many going on board?'

'The Gibbings boys, oh joy!' Exultant Suzanne has a crush on the eldest of the three, David. 'I can't wait to take off this sack and put on my new sundress, high heels, red nail polish and lippy.'

We are at the gangway now, and begin walking up the steps. Peggy, my close friend from Singapore, leans over and whispers in my ear, her green eyes dancing. 'I just saw Tony and Den Warren!' She giggles delightedly. Good-looking Tony is every girl's heart-throb, especially Peggy's. He is a few years older than us and maturing rapidly. The Warrens will disembark at Singapore and go on to Hong Kong in another ship.

When we have scrambled up the gangway and onto the spotless deck, we go in search of our cabins, which smell of fresh paint and clean linen, then check out who our companions will be in the other bunks.

Then we meet again, rush about from one deck to another, find old chums, and explore this new ship that replaced the old *Gorgon*. She is swarming now with young people: children under ten, pubescent teenagers, some girls already blossoming into pretty, curvaceous women, puppy fat gone. The Anglo-Asians are especially beautiful.

The young boys, like the younger girls, are skinny and awkward, or fat and lumpy, pimply, often freckled, with teeth missing or in braces. Some boys sound funny; their voices are breaking. Others are growing into future lady-killers.

'Hi, Fred.' I have just seen my brother with his friend, blond Edmund, who is coming to stay with us for the holidays with his sister, my friend Mollie. Fred and Edmund are eighteen and have just left Guildford Grammar School in Perth. They are fine-looking young men, well-built and lean. Fred is medium height with blue eyes and light brown hair. Edmund is taller, has blue eyes, bronze skin that he massages with coconut oil, and light blond hair. He is god-like to look at, and knows it; I have a secret crush on him, as do all the girls.

'Yramesor Eidlog, you've got fat,' Fred grimaces. We often call one another by our names spelt backwards. I like mine, it sounds exotic and Egyptian.

'You look awful yourself, Derf Eidlog.' Mortified, my face is bright red under my freckles. Any hopes for impressing Edmund, or anyone else, are dashed.

The noise on the wharf has ceased, ropes are untied, anchors rattle into place, *Gorgon*'s blue funnel gives a few deep-throated blasts signalling departure, and with the help of some tugboats it pulls away from the docks. The tugs leave as the ship negotiates Gage Roads before entering the Indian Ocean. The taste of astringent salt air and the gentle rocking of the ship mean we are on our way, with days and nights of almost unsupervised frivolity ahead of us.

The Blue Funnel Line and the 'state ships' that ply this route are true ocean liners, in miniature. *Gorgon*'s tonnage is similar to the others, three and a half thousand tons. Like Blue Funnel's

'Swingtime': Peggy Usher and me dancing in the back garden of Peggy's flat on St George's Terrace in 1938.

Centaur and *Charon* she has English officers and Chinese and Malay stewards, who go about their duties quickly and quietly in slippered feet; they meekly obey orders spoken in fluent Malay from the Singapore contingent. State ships are owned by the Western Australian government, their stewards, officers and crew are Australian. *Koolinda*, *Koolama* and *Kangaroo* sail at different times from the Blue Funnel vessels and remain only in Australian waters. Our favourite skipper, Captain Ward-Hughes, is in charge of *Gorgon*.

We line up before lunch to be sternly addressed by the two English stewardesses. Their main task is to watch over the under-tens from Java and Singapore, but they keep an eye on us too. Lifeboat drill is next and they direct us to assemble at various stations wearing our life jackets. They are boxlike and lumpy; they are not at all attractive.

About midway up the coast, *Gorgon* passes into tropical waters: the seas are a glassy turquoise, almost transparent. Schools of flying fish dart alongside us, airborne, sometimes landing on the deck. Long sulphur-yellow sea snakes float lazily near the water's surface, basking in the sunlight. Occasionally a shark fin slices through the serene ocean.

It is not always calm like this, the seas often become rough and scary. We skid down the steeply sloping decks, then climb up again to constant pitching and rolling in those days before stabilisers. During the bad weather endless green troughs of restless ocean rise into mountains, capped with foam; huge waves break over the ship's bow, she is Poseidon's toy to rock and play with. Some of us are seasick. We talk about the SS *Koombana*, which sank without a trace in 1912 out of Port Hedland; 'turned turtle', they said, in a cyclone. Charlie Chapple reassures us. 'I've heard that when you kick the bucket you see all your dead relations and friends.' Strong winds tear at our clothes and hair, seaspray tastes sharp as it whips onto the decks. In the dining saloon, tablecloths are dampened and fiddles are put up to keep settings from clattering to the floor. Portholes are tightly closed; one minute they are green with tumbling sea, the next grey with scudding clouds. The little liners are sea-worthy, though. They have been built to withstand the onslaught of howling winds and unrelenting waves.

During the day, if the weather is fine, we play deck games or sit at the ship's stern looking at the wake. When the sea is a smooth undulating pale blue, wide ribbons of a crumbly brown froth are often strewn across the surface. One boy says it's 'whales' food'. If the weather is bad we play rummy, drink squash, tease each other and read comics.

In the mid 1930s we are naïve, or most of us are, about the ways of the opposite sex. Although we have teenage 'pashes' or 'crushes', boys and girls barely touch one another. Kissing, we hear, goes on with the older ones in the shadows of lifeboats, or in them, under the stars. We are curious and ignorant. Sex is taboo until marriage; we might have a baby. Even public lava-tory seats are dangerous: you can catch venereal disease if you sit on them, so bottoms hovering, not sitting, is safest.

One day the ship heaves from side to side as she rides a heavy swell. Brian Gibbings and Peter Mackey squeeze out of their cabin porthole, wait for a slanting forty-five degree roll, then scramble along *Gorgon*'s sloping sides. They reach another row of portholes, gaining a momentary foothold, then after a fast crawl over knobbly rivets – not looking down at chasms of seething ocean – they climb up to the deck-rail. As the ship begins her rhythmic roll the other way, the boys clamber over the rail and onto the deck. They are confronted by a furious, ashen-faced captain. He has just confined Pam Gregory to her cabin for shinning up the tall blue funnel.

In the evening the girls change into simple pretty dresses, the boys into school suits, without coats. We play a wind-up gramophone on the top deck and foxtrot to Fred Astaire singing catchy songs from *Top Hat* or jive to Billy Cotton or Glenn Miller's syncopated rhythm. In between dances we sit on deckchairs.

'My mother has a red lacquer telephone in her white drawing room in Singapore,' Harold boasts, 'like Hollywood.'

'Ours hangs on the wall, we turn a handle, it rings at the Broome Post Office exchange and we talk into the brass mouthpiece,' I reply. I envy the luxuries of my Singapore friends, and the glamorous lives they will soon resume: the Swimming Club, Raffles Hotel, races, holidays in the cool Cameron Highlands where, they tell us, if you're not careful when walking in the jungle, a cobra, a krait or a tiger will kill you. They have their own *amahs*; cars driven by turbaned Indian syces; parties day and night; clothes sewn by Chinese tailors, ordered in the morning, hand-finished the same afternoon and worn that night. They shop in Orchard Road, travelling there in rickshaws pulled by coolies. Harold and Peggy's parents know the Sultan of Johore, and they are often invited to his grand dinner parties.

Peter joins us. 'Do I look different?' His face has a bare look and he says quickly before anyone can work it out, 'I've shaved off my eyebrows to make them grow bushy.'

As we near Port Hedland the intense heat begins, and we are allowed to take our bedding up onto the open deck to sleep. The captain gives instructions. 'Now girls, you sleep on this side of the deck, and boys, you bed down on the other side.' He admonishes us with a smile, 'I can see what's going on from the bridge!' At ten o'clock the stewardesses firmly tell us it's time for bed, or we'll look sickly and overtired when our parents see us.

We strip our bunks and roll up our mattresses and sheets; in pyjamas and light dressing-gowns we clamber up companion-ways to the open deck again. Even at sea there is no coolness in the wind; it blows hot, humid and boisterous over us. As we climb the steps kimonos fly open, silk pyjamas cling, outlining maturing bodies, some newly voluptuous.

'The boys can see *everything*!' I say, feeling self-conscious.

'Don't worry about it, Bud.' Suzanne grins mischievously, the others chuckle; they don't care so I decide not to either.

The night is stifling hot as we try to sleep under a sky lit to indigo by masses of brilliant stars; the ocean is black, except for the brilliant paths where *Gorgon*'s lights shine on foam-marbled green water as the ship cleaves its way onwards. Sleeping on deck is infinitely better than lying in an airless cabin, stuffy even with an electric table fan.

After breakfast the next day – cereal, eggs, buttered toast – we walk up the wide stairway from the dining saloon. We'll soon be in Port Hedland where Suzanne will be leaving us. We can see mangrove trees on either side of the ship now.

Suzanne lives on a cattle station near Marble Bar – the

hottest place on earth, it's said. Her home is the size of a small European country. 'See you when we go back to school!' She runs to her cabin to finish packing. We're on deck trying to catch a breeze. Fred comes over.

'It won't be long before we tie up at the jetty.' Hearing this, we all sprint to our cabins, find some money, and gather in groups as *Gorgon* glides towards the wharf. The ship bells ring, crewmen pound along the deck in a hurry; after several minutes of shouting, *Gorgon* ties up. We wait for the gangway to be lowered.

Everyone goes ashore and strolls around the small town in the searing, dry heat; it seems lifeless, but a cafe is open. Some of us step into its dark interior and ask for 'spiders'. We grasp cold glasses of cordial with scoops of vanilla ice-cream floating on top, then we sit down and stir the luscious combination with our straws. The potion froths and dribbles down the tall sides of our glasses. Walking back, someone suggests a swim in the pool. It is shark-netted and close to the wharf.

The ship is due to arrive in Broome the next day. Pam says, 'We'll go to Cable Beach on Sunday and everyone can come back to our house afterwards.' It's party time.

That night we pack, then crowd into the lounge bar, drink ginger beer, lemonade and creaming soda. The Singaporeans sign chits that their parents will pay. We dare not, so we use the last of our pocket money.

In the bright blue morning *Gorgon* cannot berth at Broome's long jetty: if she does she'll miss the tide and be stranded high and dry on wet grey mud for hours, upsetting her schedule.

Wearing our best clothes so we look good to meet our families, the Broome passengers step gingerly down the swaying gangway, carrying our hand luggage. There is a slight swell, a seaman helps us jump into a bobbing lifeboat manned by two crew and a young officer in white uniform; our trunks have been stacked in the boat already. Our friends still on board lean over the railing and wave goodbye. The lifeboat, with its motor going, takes us over the rolling water.

We near the jetty and see a large group of people, looking at first like dots of bright confetti in the distance; now closer. Fred and I see Mother, Father and our young sister, Daisy. Beautiful Mother – musical, literate, articulate – is waving joyfully; she is loving and greatly loved. Dad has to be negotiated carefully; Daisy is an admiring little sister with ready laughter.

We leave the lifeboat, climbing onto the jetty's lower landing, and walk up the wet wooden steps to noisily greet our families and friends.

We introduce Mollie and Edmund to our parents, who welcome them warmly and ask our school chums to call them Aunty Doris and Uncle Lou instead of Captain and Mrs Goldie: they will be staying with us as members of the family for many weeks to come. This familiar form of address is acceptable among all our friends, so no-one is embarrassed. Mollie and Edmund's parents are Aunty Jean and Uncle Guy to Fred and me; we often spend holidays with them on their wheat farm at Dangin.

We begin to walk down the half-mile-long wooden jetty with everyone else, chattering, laughing and full of excitement.

Cars are parked at the other end to take us home. Luggage will follow in the old steam train with its open carriages and goods trucks. It is only used when a ship anchors at the jetty.

Our house, La Bonbonnière, meaning a sweet box or doll's house, is a typical master pearler's bungalow. Like a doll's house it is not; perhaps my mother named it thus to point out the stark differences between it and her stately home, New Farm, in England. Though our house is airy and high-ceilinged, it's not at all flimsy or delicate as its name suggests. Like all pearlers' bungalows, it's built like a ship, constructed by Malay and Japanese carpenters, who use timber left over from crafting pearling masters' luggers – teak, jarrah, mahogany, Oregan pine. Decks become verandahs, amidships the central rooms, shutters are sails. The solid dark-wood house is secured against raging cyclones by steel cables crossing over the iron roof and into strong anchor-hooks dug deeply into the ground.

Low wooden lattice fences surround the verandahs on two sides of the house, and are shaded by half-open shutters. Our dining room is near the kitchen at one end of the spacious west-facing verandah; at right angles to the dining area the verandah widens to accommodate a variety of comfortable cane chairs, assorted tables and a chaise longue, the furniture imported from nearby Singapore. Jarrah-timbered walls are dark-stained; a handsome brass ship's clock and barometer hang next to a black German helmet with its fearsome head-spike, a trophy that Dad brought home from the Great War. Our old-fashioned telephone hangs on the wall, too. On the jarrah floor is an expanse of coconut matting. We call this place the sitting room.

At the other end of the dining verandah is a long room filled with beds, well spaced, like a dormitory, stretching along the width of the house. It is enclosed by fine steel mesh: this is the mosquito room, nearly every house in Broome has one. We sleep here all year round except for the cooler months between May and September, when we sleep in our bedrooms in the middle of the house. Fred has his own room on the opposite side, built like a captain's cabin on a small liner with double bunk beds, a desk and bookshelves. The mesh keeps out ferocious mosquitoes that inject fevers as they suck blood; plaguey flies can't get in, and neither can flesh-nipping sandflies, sting-ing hornets and scorpions. Full-length iron shutters, slightly elevated, shield our mosquito room from the weather. Electric fans placed near our beds make the sweltering nights more bearable; their droning noise is soothing.

Another verandah at the back, cluttered with ropes, tackle and sacks, is enclosed by lattice; our Japanese cook Tora's bed-room opens from it – this is his domain. Separating our living

Our house, La Bonbonnière,
in the 1930s.

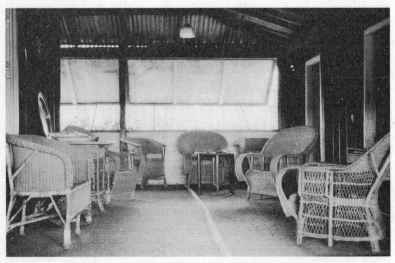

Our verandah sitting room.

area from Tora's are the bathroom, Dad's office, the kitchen and the storeroom. The storeroom is the size of a small grocery shop. Shelves are filled with survival food as well as some luxuries like Edgell's canned white asparagus and Nestlé's tinned cream, necessities for household cleaning, medicines and hard chewing tobacco for the Aborigines. We wait eagerly for the steamer each fortnight to replenish our storeroom, and deliver goods ordered from Perth that aren't available from the merchants in Japtown – such as magazines, make-up and ready-made clothes.

The lavatory is outside, down the back steps, a short walk away. A wooden screen riotous with bougainvillea conceals the stout timber structure containing a long wooden seat with a hole, a can underneath and squares of paper on a string nailed to the wall. Two muscular brown 'sanitary' men in khaki clothes come twice a week to take away the full cans, which they balance on their shoulders, and replace with empty, disinfected ones. No-one in Broome has a flushing lavatory. During the night we use chamber-pots that are kept under our beds.

Once when I was walking in bare feet on the hot orange earth towards the lavatory, Dad shouted from the back door: 'Buddy, put on shoes at once. I've told you before, this soil is full of hookworm. It burrows into the soles of your feet and up into your body; there's no cure.' I never went barefoot outside again.

The Aboriginal gardener, Jerry, and his wife, our maid Topsy, live in the well built but bare room behind the lavatory. I've furtively looked inside, and wonder if the smell of our outhouse worries them. Where do they keep their clothes, where and what do they eat? The floorboards are bare and the walls are empty, clean, blank. Perhaps they do not live in their shed at all, but with other Aborigines in the camp next door.

Our house sits on cement blocks capped with tin to control predatory white ants, dry rot and entry by reptiles. Although a snake once found its way into the storeroom, and was eventually dispatched by Dad and Tora. Bright green croaking frogs sometimes sit on Mother's dressing table among her polished silver hairbrushes, hand mirror, button hook and shoehorn. At night fat black cockroaches, thick on the floorboards of the kitchen and back verandah, ooze white 'blood' when we accidentally step on them.

The Aborigines' camp is beside us on Guy Street, and they are mostly peaceable neighbours. We live side by side, but have little to do with each other, though some of the Aborigines work at odd jobs as gardeners and maids. Mother and Dad have a 'live and let live' philosophy, although we hardly see the Aborigines next door as there is so much space between us. I often fall asleep to the rhythmic tapping of clapsticks, or the melancholy wailing of a traditional song.

Most of the blocks of land around us on Guy and Walcott streets are empty, but there is a small cottage opposite our house and further down the road is the Masonic Hall. The other master pearlers have bungalows like ours, all on the sparsely covered fringes of town; many have lovely gardens. It would be a long, hot and dusty walk over the ridge to the commercial centre of Broome – Japtown, as locals and visitors alike call it; we always go by car.

Broome is like an island, cut off by dense grey bush, separated by endless red desert – pindan – on one side and vast unpredictable ocean on the other. It is the most isolated town on the continent, perched on the edge of the north-west coast, more Asian than Australian. Broome is closer to Java than to Perth, its population is multicultural, an exotic mixture of races – Asian, European and Indigenous – lured here since 1861 by the pioneers of pearl-fishing. Nature is untamed; white man is living in a hostile environment. It is a challenge, the land and the ocean waiting to be conquered by adventurous males, but it is a difficult place for most women of European birth. Only Aboriginal people understand this country – it is both mother and father to them, revered and loved. They are part of it, and have no wish to conquer, change or wrest a fortune from it or the surrounding sea.

At times, an age-old telepathy summons them to 'go walk-about'. It is immediate; they are here with us one day, gone the next. An invisible beam calls them to a faraway place. I am conscious of their connection with the spiritual and natural worlds; Topsy has told me of mysterious events known only to her people. Both Topsy and Jerry go walkabout now and then for weeks on end, and we have to find other people to fill in for them while they're away.

Christmas is the hottest time of the year in Broome. It is cyclone and storm time; 'lay-up' for pearling fleets, when it's too dangerous for boats to go to sea; days and nights of sticky humidity with a brassy daytime sky. Every evening sheet lightning flashes and distant thunder mutters. There are nights when, without warning, ominous clouds suddenly loom and a 'cock-eye-bob' explodes overhead. Rain buckets down, blown in all directions by shrieking winds. If we are at the open-air Sun Pictures cinema when the storm hits we have to rush for the covered part and wait till it passes. Or when we are asleep in the middle of the night, at the first bombardment of rain on the iron roof and cracking thunderclaps, Dad jumps from his bed in the mosquito room, shouts for Tora in his quarters at the other end of the house and to any other men who are staying with us. They rush around outside, swearing, crashing shutters down to stop the wind-driven rain from swamping the verandahs. The storm is over quickly; then outside all is serenely still, the stars are blazing, and it's a little cooler.

It is time for a swim at Cable Beach. Mollie, Edmund, Fred and I love the beach. With Fred at the wheel, 'Greengage', our 1933 Essex with a dicky seat at the back, rockets along the red-dirt track through scrub, grey and monotonous. We have our bathing suits on. Mollie's and mine are the latest fashion, one-pieces in blue. We have swimming caps, which we wear whenever we go in the water. After twenty minutes the car emerges onto a high bluff overlooking deserted white sand stretching pristine below us; beyond is the kingfisher-blue Indian Ocean. It is monsoon season and the waves along the thirteen-mile stretch of Cable Beach look to me like towering monsters driven by devilish forces; crashing and roaring, usually too turbulent for cruising sharks. The grown-ups love it, and some of the youngsters, good swimmers, enjoy the buffeting. I don't because I can't swim, but love pretending to surf in the shallows.

I've been scared of Cable Beach waves as long as I can remember. When I was eleven, and small for my age, handsome Captain Ancell Gregory – father of my friend Pam and known universally as 'Greg' – tried to teach me to surf. 'Come on, Bud, you'll have to learn, I'll take you out with me,' he said. I said, 'No, thank you,' but he won. We walked out towards the terrifying maelstrom, right into the middle of the surging breakers. Tall and powerful, a legendary survivor of shipwreck in cyclonic seas, swimming for days before being washed up on a beach, Greg suddenly lost his balance as a mighty wave nearly toppled us, but he regained his foothold and all was well, though I was white and rigid with alarm. Of course, he wanted me to conquer my fear, but I never learned to surf. Pam is like her adored father, fearless, a dolphin in the water, and champion swimmer for her school, Perth College.

The others are not scared at all: they've plunged straight out into the surf. There are other reasons I avoid going out; the beach is empty most of the time, never patrolled, and there is no shark net as there is at Town Beach. I have seen the odd shark cruising around.

After our swim Edmund has a turn at driving and brings us home. We put on clean shorts and shirts after tepid bore-water showers, and sit down together with Mother, Daisy and Dad around the massive table Dad's carpenter has crafted from the same teak that is used in building luggers. Mother looks fresh in a flowered cotton dress, Daisy wears shorts like us, my father is in his around-the-house rig: khaki shorts and open-neck shirt revealing curling ginger chest-hair.

Dad is a master pearler, has a fleet of pearling luggers, employs Asian crewmen, specialist carpenters, Japanese divers. It is lay-up, the monsoon season from November to March, a time of sudden crashing storms and deadly willy-willies. Just now he is in fine form, ready to tell stories of pearls and adventures at sea, and his life in the Dutch East Indies as a young man. We are eager to help ourselves to ice-cold crayfish, crabs and prawns – Tora has heaped them onto flat dishes and spread them out on the table.

The shellfish were caught yesterday at Barred Creek, and delivered in a damp heaving sack that evening by Toshi, the Japanese fisherman. They are boiled at once on the four-burner kerosene stove, green and alive, claws and whiskers agitating until cooked and bright pink. Tora is used to the job. He drains them in the wooden sink and chills the catch in the ice chest. Handsome Jim Milner delivers big slabs of ice every morning and afternoon. He races into the house carrying the dripping block with iron tongs, puts it in the ice chest, then leaves in his truck. Jim is twenty and owns the iceworks with his father; he makes ginger beer, lemonade and creaming soda too.

A double loaf of white bread from the town baker is on the table with a long knife; tinned butter from our storeroom looks presentable in flowered dishes. The wireless is tuned in to lunchtime music at the Hotel des Indes in Batavia, Java. It's heavenly listening to the ensembles, sweet music coming over the airwaves, and we feel part of the sophisticated crowd in the hotel's elegant dining room. Dad was there in his bachelor gadabout days; he has fond memories of the place. Above the table a ceiling fan is switched on to full speed, stirring hot air, making it seem cooler. Cicadas shrill loudly outside. Our plates are full; Daisy, the youngest, says grace. Dad spreads melting butter on his bread, wipes perspiration from his forehead in spite of the fan.

Fred, with his penchant for unusual facts and figures, regales our guests with a risqué tidbit of information: pearl oysters are hermaphrodites. Mollie and I nod, showing we understand, turn to one another, agree quietly we're glad we're not oysters. Like all males, Edmund and Fred are fascinated with anything to do with pearling. The conversation becomes technical as they pester Dad with questions. I'm glad Fred isn't showing off his knowledge too much; Dad has been known to interrupt him testily with, 'Burble burble burble.' He can't bear academic talk at his table; he has to be top male, the old instinctive head of the herd.

Tuning out, I think of a pearl-shell's beauty when the rough exterior has been smoothed away, and each half brushed to a sheen. A polished mother-of-pearl shell makes an unusual holder for letters, pins, jewellery, or just as an ornament. I look over to the sitting room where half a lustrous shell, silver as moonlight, lies reflecting the light on a burnished brass table.

Ah Wong, Dad's old Chinese cook on the lugger *Rosef*, once

told me that in certain parts of China, mother-of-pearl shell is shaved until transparent, and used as windowpanes. I imagine living inside a fantasy pavilion and gazing out at a magical world misted in a pearl glow.

I have seen glossy pearl-shells with flower gardens carved into them by local Japanese men, and I do not like the fussy cluttered look of them. But Dad tells us of Thursday Island's sacred neck ornaments made of fretted pearl-shell, the *zogo mai*, which are worn at ceremonies by the natives. We see a sketch of one, the design a filigree of symmetrical cubes and circles; it is enchanting.

Mother helps Daisy fork meat from a crab claw. She touches her graduated matching pearl necklace, luminous against her milky skin. Her English complexion is unblemished by the tropical sun; she guards it by wearing a shady hat when she goes outside. Fred and I know that Dad's fishing for pearl-shell and the occasional pearl pays our boarding-school fees, as well as building our pearler's bungalow. We understand, but never mention, that far away in England, Grandpa and Granny help with expenses at bad times like last year's disastrous willy-willy. It is their way of easing the harshness of life for their daughter in this frontier town.

The pearls glow as Mother talks, her blue-green eyes glow too. She smiles at us in her charming way and adds her mite of wisdom: 'Pearls are a feminine jewel, women should wear them during the day as well as in the evening; they are not showy like diamonds.' The boys pull long faces, they are bored now, but Mollie and I listen intently. We love jewellery, our favourite film

*Tora in our Broome garden
in the 1930s.*

stars, Jean Harlow and Ginger Rogers, wear pearls in all the movie magazines. Mollie is envious: Dad has shown her the pearls he is putting aside to make into a necklace for my twenty-first birthday. 'Human skin keeps pearls shining . . . if they're put away and never worn they grow dull and lifeless.' Mother ignores the boys and removes a jade-green grasshopper from her plate; the gyrating fan usually blows away winged insects.

Tora appears, smiling, with the last plate of shellfish and takes away two tureens full of scraps.

'Thank you, Tora san, all taste very good.' Mother is pleased to have Tora helping full-time in the kitchen. Thin and wiry, Tora could be any age from thirty to fifty. He has spiky black hair and yellow teeth that he whistles through a lot; he rattles saucepans and patters around in thongs. He wears his khaki trousers half-mast, rolled up at the bottom, a wide cummerbund round his waist to keep the pants up. Tora has a wife and son in

Japan; I know because I used to watch him write letters to them. I was fascinated by the Japanese characters, written right to left. He visited them once, when we were in England, but he never talks about them. He has regular flare-ups with 'Boss' (my father), and disappears for several days to Japtown, to gambling and opium dens. We know he's back when we smell burning toast, hear scraping noises in the morning and find the table laid for breakfast. Tora stands in the kitchen doorway with his wide ingratiating grin. Like Mother, we children are always pleased to see him back.

Dad takes the plate and passes it around the table. Mollie thinks she will have one more large delectable prawn. The boys finish what's left while we go on talking and laughing. Everyone is contented. At two o'clock we are ready to relax on our beds for the customary afternoon siesta. Tora is hovering impatiently now, not smiling, clicking his teeth. He wants to clear away, wash up and lie down too.

Mother, Dad and Daisy put on kimonos and go to the mosquito room for siesta. Mollie and I loll on white-sheeted beds at the other end of the big room and talk softly about our favourite boys and tonight's dance at the Reynolds' house. Fred and Edmund walk barefoot from the table over to large cane chairs and sit down.

Broome gives up in early afternoon during the monsoon season; there are no signs of life in Japtown or in the rest of our sprawling community until three-thirty, except for the Aborigines. In their camp next door, men and women sit on tomato-red earth under gaunt gum trees, brush away flies, slap mosquitoes, chatter while playing cards; children lie about talking together, their large brown eyes covered with flies; no-one brushes them away. Even the Aborigines' kangaroo-dogs stretch out in whatever shade there is, bite at fleas and sandflies, flick flies with their tails and snooze.

Palm fronds hang limply outside. Flowering oleanders grow along our boundaries – crimson, pink, apricot, white, singles and doubles, their musky sweet scent permeates the air, almost overpowering the fragrance of ripe mangoes. The poinciana tree is smothered in flamboyant scarlet and yellow flowers; magenta bougainvillea reverberates with blazing colour under full sun. Pink banana blossoms drip nectar in the heat; sometimes I can't resist sipping from them.

The tall bird-of-paradise hedge has dense ferny foliage, a cool lime-green contrasting with its orange pea-flower plumes massed along the top. Mother is proud of the hedge, it hides the chicken-run too. The restful screen fills the gap between half-open shutters and verandah railings, fiery blooms out of sight.

Gardens in the Tropic of Capricorn are quite different from

European gardens. The colours are nearly all bright primary and the flower scents are strong, sometimes overpowering. It is a world away from the subtly perfumed, gently coloured tapestry of flowers at our grandparents' house, New Farm, in Kent. Fred, Daisy and I spent delightful years of our childhood there with Mother, Granny and Grandpa, while Dad tended to the business in Broome. Now we are home with him for good, but we miss New Farm terribly.

The tropical vegetation was a shock to my mother, a young sheltered English woman, when she first came to Australia, especially combined with the impact of Broome's extraordinary landscape and primitive living standards. To her it was like landing on another planet after the month-long sea journey from Britain through the Suez Canal, then another week-long sea trip from Fremantle to Broome.

Our garden in the nor'west of Australia is my father's domain. After the house was built between 1919 and 1920, the sweltering heat had already enervated Mother, and she was pregnant with my sister Dolly. My brother Fred was two, so she was only too glad for Dad to take over. She couldn't be inspired by exotic tropical plants she knew nothing about.

In the time he had at home between going to sea with his pearling luggers, Dad organised the layout and clearing of the scrubby double block on the corner of Walcott and Guy streets. He worked hard with help from Jerry, the Aboriginal gardener, even though he was in constant pain from terrible war wounds and was mentally scarred as well, making him difficult to cope with.

Dad and Jerry planted the hedge of bird-of-paradise that Mother loves, tend the lemon and pomelo trees and rear mango trees with great success. We have several kinds called by their common names: 'peach' and 'apple' mango are two of them; stringy 'turpentine' mangoes have no place in our garden. Mother invented her special dessert 'Mango Cream' from the best fruit. She slices flesh from the stones into a bowl, hand-squeezes out the rest of the pulp and juice, adds Nestlé's tinned cream – there is no fresh cream in Broome – then mashes all ingredients together until smooth. The mixture is put into tall-stemmed glasses in the ice chest – soon to be replaced with a kerosene fridge – to set firm and luscious. The concoction is served chilled at evening parties, with more dollops of Nestlé's cream. After dinner we sit around the massive teak table under the whirling ceiling fan, eating this wonderful sweet, the daytime-shrilling cicadas now giving occasional chirps, the warm breeze rustling the long pandanus leaves. The Aborigines in their camp next door click ceremonial clapsticks or dance their corroborees while sheet lightning flickers constantly across dazzling stars.

Dad has a passion for growing different kinds of tomatoes among the lemons and pomelos, and they are full of flavour. My favourite is a big oblong tomato with thin pale pink skin, the flesh sweet and juicy. It flourishes in Broome's fiery red soil.

Coconut palms bear green-husked fruit. When it's cut open you see the skull-like brown hairy shell surrounding the coconut's inside that we use in different ways – in cooking, or the fresh brittle flesh broken into portions and crunched on with relish. Jerry shins his way up the trunk to the cluster of fruit, cuts one away with a knife, then it falls to the ground. One day Dad created a concoction that may or may not have been a success with his friends. I remember Jerry climbing the tree and throwing down an unripe coconut; we trooped into the kitchen and watched Dad hack it open. Inside, the flesh was a white jelly . . . we each scooped out a spoonful, which tasted rather nice; the liquid a clear greenish colour. Dad poured the coconut water into an empty steel-meshed soda siphon, put a blanket around it in his usual manner in case it blew up, then he shook and shook, prancing about until the liquid was aerated. He normally used tank-rainwater for soda water. That night Dad and the other men in their whites, the women in pretty dresses, gathered for five o'clock drinks on our verandah, comfortable in cane armchairs, and tried the sparkling coconut soda in their whiskies. I don't know the reaction, but there were always choices which the men enjoyed mixing – gimlets, gin bitters and iced water or soda with lots of ice, Singapore slings, cold beer.

Pandanus, too, does well in Broome as the climate is right; they grow throughout South-East Asia and the Pacific islands. We don't use the leaves in cooking, but the Asians in town do; they enjoy the flavour it gives their food and the unique grass-green colour it lends to their cakes. We grow our pandanus as ornamental plants on each side of the front door, their long roughish leaves reach upwards before falling like a green fountain brushing the edge of the front steps; they sway and rustle in a breeze. The pandanus are cut back occasionally to stop their skinny trunks from growing too tall, showing their ugly aerial roots. Our pandanus make an effective exotic screen, but we always have to watch out for snakes where leaves hide the sides of the wooden steps or fall onto the crushed shell path. Mother was bitten once, as she waved goodbye to us as we left for a party. Dad saved her life, cauterising the bite and applying hot poultices to the wound for days afterwards to draw out the venom. I remember Mother screamed with the pain.

Broome is alive with snakes. There are plenty of them here, various types, and poisonous: the desert death adder, the brown snake, the king brown, the black snake, the copperhead. We've warned Mollie and Edmund to be prepared: 'If you see a snake, stare at it – it mesmerises them.' We don't stand too near any low-lying bushes and we never go outside at night without a torch. Whenever I am lying inside having a rest, I keep an eye out through the mosquito wire; often I see snakes streaking out from under the house and slithering across the grass to the bush.

Lemongrass is another Asian staple that grows well in Broome, flavouring traditional dishes and used as medicine; a clump grows in our garden and we sometimes add the subtle lemony-tasting stems to our own European cooking.

Since our house, like everyone else's, is perched on termite-proof cement blocks, rows of vincas (the Madagascar periwinkle) have been planted to hide the under-house gap. The flowers are pale and anaemic-looking, washed-out white and a sickly mauve. I don't like them. More to my taste is the frangipani tree growing by the side verandah steps, carrying clusters of delicately fragrant creamy-gold flowers. Like all the girls in Broome, I pick one to wear behind my ear. Dad is delighted; he says I look like his sister Daisy.

One day as a small child I remember standing still and looking up at an enormous yellow-gold sunflower, taller than me and with a friendly face; always inquisitive, I stared into its huge centre of dark brown seeds. The sunflower and I communed for some time; I have always felt close to the elemental world of nature, and this flower in our Broome garden I like best of all.

Fred has studied hard during his final year, surprising us – but not Mother. He has won the Western Australia gold medal for English, a scholarship to the Royal Military College, Duntroon, in Canberra, and another to the University of Western Australia with private rooms at St George's College. He plans to study law. His headmaster has just sent a telegram to say that Fred is short-listed for this year's Rhodes scholarship. Everyone is excited.

Edmund isn't as academically inclined as Fred, though he has no trouble passing exams. He and Mollie's family own a baby-food company in England, but their English father prefers to live in Australia on their wheat farm near York. Ed plans to leave Australia and work in the family company next year. Mollie and I still have a few years of school ahead of us: right now our post-school plans are hazy and revolve more around parties and fun than careers and employment. Daisy already shows signs of challenging Fred's tacit title of brains of the family.

At four o'clock we gather at the table for afternoon tea, sitting in our usual places, fan switched on again. Fred and Ed have just returned from another swim, this time at Town Beach, ten minutes walk away. Even as a little girl, I would walk there with my friends during the day and play hopscotch in the sand when the tide was out, or walk round the rocks picking up strange and beautiful shells. Sometimes we collect oysters, cutting the clenched shells open with our knives. We know to collect only from live shells washed over by seawater and still wet. Those we don't eat we put into billycans to take home.

Above where Town Beach begins is Broome's half-mile-long wooden jetty; it starts high on the tumbled red rocks rising from the blinding white sand at one end of the beach, stretches out with a curve, straightens again and stops abruptly to meet the ocean at high tide. We walk to its end and back many times. The steam engine with a few open carriages attached only runs when a ship docks, but most people prefer to walk anyway, both young and old, day or night, cooler weather or scorching hot. I remember only once sitting in a carriage when I was too young to walk the distance. On bright moonlit nights when the tide is right, fishing from the jetty is popular with everyone,

*The Broome township at the
top of Roebuck Bay in the early 1900s.*

*The old Broome jetty, to the left of Town Beach,
with two ships in port.*

especially the Aborigines, who know more than anyone else about catching fish. They stand in groups in embrasures all the way along, their piles of glistening silver fish continually growing. We know they have a special knowledge, an extra sense between their hands, the line, the bait, of when to tug and tantalise, when to pull in the catch. We walk to the jetty's end and down to the less dangerous lower platform where we throw out our lines and wait. Some have a knack and are rewarded, although no-one ever matches the Aborigines.

Mother, Dad and Daisy have slept while the boys swam. Mollie and I, excited about tonight's party, haven't stopped talking. Mother pours tea for the adults and the boys; Daisy, Mollie and I drink glasses of fresh goat's milk, considered more nutritious than milk from the cows that graze near Broome on poor feed. I love the pure, nutty taste. The milk comes from our goat, which is tethered in the bush opposite. Mother pays our teenage neighbour, Anna, to milk her for us. We hand around silver dishes of hot toast-fingers thickly buttered. Tora nearly always burns the toast. When we smell scorching, hear scraping and curses from the kitchen, we know it's time for tea.

Fred tells us he saw two big sea-eagles circling the steep red cliffs towering above the beach. Broome teems with wildlife – the parrots and cockatoos are the noisiest. Kangaroos don't venture into town much, but they are everywhere in the bush.

There is rustling among the dense long-leaved pandanus trees on either side of the open front door a few feet from us. Alert, we listen, is it a snake?

Now we hear footsteps crunch on the shell-grit front path,

the tread of shoe-leather ascending wooden steps: a pith helmet appears in the doorway; we see the sunburnt face and tall figure of Uncle Mac. A distinguished-looking man, he wears spotless white, his old-fashioned jacket buttoned to the neck. At heel is Nipper, a wire-haired fox terrier, Uncle Mac's faithful follower and friend.

'Uncle Mac!' We're excited, he's a favourite. Dad jumps to his feet.

Mac smiles at Fred and me. 'Good to see the children home from school; a year's a long time, they've changed, grown up.' He speaks slowly, perfect diction, a deep voice. He's tall as a Viking, six feet five inches.

J. T. C. Mackenzie is one of Broome's gentleman-desperadoes. Like all of them, the nonconformist within is hidden by a highly civilised exterior. He's made a fortune or two, and lost them. He's pearled in the Dutch East Indies and Australian waters. He skippered the schooner *Alice*, bringing a fleet of thirty-six luggers from the Aru Islands, and was wrecked at dusk on a reef by the man at the wheel, who mistook the barely visible rocks for a low mist. Uncle Mac and some of the crew survived three days clinging to masts until two men in a rowboat reached Beagle Bay, a hundred miles away, and rescue came.

Mackenzie's claim to fame was finding the 'Star of the West', one of the most magnificent pearls ever seen, while directing 'Pearl King' James Clark's fleet off Willie Creek. It is the size of a sparrow's egg, pear-shaped, perfect in colour and lustre. It sold for about £10,000, a fortune, to a pearl buyer named Sussman, and was later displayed in Melbourne where such a crowd came to see it that they had to be controlled by police. Later the pearl was sold in London for an undisclosed price.

Uncle Mac is an intriguing mystery to me. Like many men from privileged families and civilised cultures, he is seduced by Broome. It is a last outpost, a man's town, no cold winters, and almost – but not completely – cut off. All here are identities, but dependent on one another, with pearlers socially at the top. Everyone else is respectful, including the vast Asian population. A white master pearler is a big fish in a small pond. The lifestyle is free and easy, though conventions are still observed in the evening: changing for drinks and dinner, immaculate clothes fresh from the *dhobi*.

Uncle Mac, with Nipper, lives on 'the foreshore' like a beachcomber, a wrecked lugger, spindrift. I have never seen his house, or hut, if he has one. Like other pearlers who refused to leave Broome when times were bad – world markets began rejecting pearl-shell around the start of World War I in favour of the new, cheaper synthetics – Mackenzie stayed on. His wife and children left long ago. Gentle, kind, sombre Uncle Mac, the man we know with his clean, frayed collars and polished shoes, is a welcome dinner guest each week at the Goldies', Normans', Lyons' and other families. He is a fountain of pearling lore and stories, but he's come to talk to Dad about the new threat to their livelihood and Broome's prosperity – the Japanese cultured pearl business. Dad is disparaging; the artificial pearls will never have the lasting quality of natural ones, he declares, nor the sense of romance and adventure. But we know that some pearlers fear that resident Japanese in Broome are planning to copy the method, thereby consolidating their power. Pam's father Greg is one of the few who sees a future for the 'artificial' pearls.

In my mind our English grandmother is also a fairy godmother. Every ship from Perth brings large parcels from England. Once a month Mother looks forward to the latest English magazines, lengths of beautiful material, a fashionable new dress. Granny has sent me a green organdie party frock embroidered with white eyelet-hole flowers: it's slimming, cut on the cross with an ankle-length hem; silver sandals with little heels give me height. It is hard to get clothes like this in Broome, though sometimes we buy material from the Chinese draper in Japtown and Elée Bardwell makes up the dresses. Mollie has gold sandals and a long dress of white crepe made by her mother.

Afternoon tea over, Mollie and I go to my room to see what we'll need for tonight's dance. My room is quite bare; I only sleep in it in the winter. I keep my clothes in here, and have a white dressing table, where I keep all my make-up and my silver dressing-table set from England, and a bookcase. We bring the ironing board into the sitting room to press our dresses while we talk to Fred and Edmund, who are lounging in cane chairs. Mollie smooths creases in her white dress with the iron. She thinks Fred is good-looking.

'Fred, will you have a favourite dance partner tonight?' She is flippant and rather flirtatious.

'I like Rhoda Reynolds with her pointed chin and black eyes, but she's always with Jim Kennedy. Don't think I've a chance. I'll look around when we get there.' He stretches and yawns.

Mollie grimaces at me, then says it's my turn for the iron. Slipping my green dress onto the board and dashing the iron over it I feel a bit cheeky. 'Ed, you've kept quiet, have you seen anyone nice yet? I've noticed lots of girls talking to you.'

'Wait and see.' The boys are not giving anything away, and ignore our jaunty quizzing.

Ironing finished, it's time for showers, cleaning teeth; girls first then boys. The shower is above the bathtub, and we shower in the reddish, metallic-smelling bore water. The tank water is reserved for drinking and cooking. The water is never heated; in Broome there is never any need.

In the bedroom, Mollie and I splash Evening in Paris perfume on our bodies, add clouds of talcum powder with the same scent, retrieve silk underwear from huge screw-top jars, used to protect them from hungry moths and silverfish eager to chew it into holes overnight. We put on as much Max Factor make-up as we dare, first spitting on cakes of black mascara, stirring it to a paste with its brush, then stroking the sticky substance onto our eyelashes until they curl. We like it because it is the same make-up as the movie stars wear. We outline stretched lips with bright pink lipstick. Our hair is brushed and burnished, wound around fingers to make soft corkscrew curls, which hang over our shoulders. Ready for our party finery, we step into our dresses and slip our feet into sandals. Though Mother always wears silk stockings when she goes out to afternoon tea, we rarely do. It is just too hot.

At seven o'clock we meet our brothers, who are wearing semi-formal outfits acceptable for young men in tropical climates: white trousers, casual white shirts, shining black shoes. Their hair is sleeked down with Yardley's Old English Lavender brilliantine. Then we assemble for Mother's inspection. Fred fetches her from the side verandah where she has been sitting with Daisy, talking about scholarship exams to Perth Modern School and to St Hilda's.

'Ready, Mum.'

Mother smiles delightedly and carefully examines the four of us. 'Boys, I'm proud of you. How fresh and smart you are.'

Focusing on Mollie and me she has reservations. 'Girls, you look very pretty in your new dresses and I like your long curls. But you're wearing too much make-up.'

'Oh, Mum, everyone wears make-up.'

'Very well, this once.'

Little Daisy is envious. 'Wish I was old enough to go too.'

I console her: 'Your turn will come when we're old hags.'

Mother kisses us. 'Dad is waiting for you in the garage, and remember, Tom Peters has borrowed his father's tabletop truck and is bringing you home after the party. Now run along, darlings, and enjoy yourselves.'

Tora is leaning against the kitchen doorjamb, grinning broadly and approvingly. 'His' family will do him justice tonight. The Reynolds' 'Number One' dance is the talk of Broome, from Sheba Lane to Carnarvon Street, along the foreshores and in the pubs. Mr Reynolds is Broome's Government Resident and Magistrate. He goes to the courthouse every day, and is at the top of the local hierarchy, except for the master pearlers who hold a unique – and exalted – position in the community.

'You all-same first-class passengers tonight.' Tora's opinion of people is summed up by being, in his eyes, first- or second-class passengers.

On a wave of admiration we file through the kitchen to the back verandah, and out the back door into the night.

Walking on the cooling red earth down to the garage, we hear the car's motor throbbing evenly. We girls squeeze in front; the boys spring into the dicky seat at the back. We are off, headlights blazing as we travel unlit roads. The only streetlights are in Japtown.

The Reynolds live in a comfortable bungalow surrounded by wide verandahs, opposite the Bishop's Palace and set apart from the closely settled town. The Residency's green lawns roll right to the edge of a high cliff overlooking the azure waters of Roebuck Bay. There are several children in the family, ranging in age from four to eighteen. Gordon is the eldest boy, a little older than me, tall, good-looking; we are attracted to each other.

We leave the car and thank Dad for driving us. Gordon greets me as we walk towards the house. Mollie wonders whether to favour dashing Nolan McDaniel or his quieter cousin, Graham Bardwell, as they rush to meet her. All the boys at the party are dressed in tropical whites. Fred and Edmund are the centre of attention in no time; girls, like colourful butterflies, flutter around them as they climb the front steps.

Entering the house we see Pam Gregory, ravishing in red slipper satin. Pam, with her elfin face, cap of soft brown hair and twinkling eyes, a lovely girl–woman, is my childhood friend; we have played together since we were babies and our parents are best friends. Now her parents are separated. She lives for ten months of the year with her elegant mother in a big house overlooking the Swan River, goes to Perth College and leads a conventional life. Christmas holidays have meant travelling by ship to Broome and her father since she was seven years old. Parents know that the stewardesses are experienced in caring for the child-passengers. Dashing pearling master, Captain Ancell Gregory, is admired by men and loved by many women. He has style and is a unique, colourful, elegant individual; a legend already, from Fremantle to Darwin. He is very well-spoken, speaks Malay, and even imports his own brand of Egyptian cigarettes.

Captain Gregory treats his daughter as an equal and she is his hostess. They employ a Chinese houseboy, an Aboriginal maid, Regina, and assorted part-time staff. Now that she is fifteen Pam supervises the cooking and prepares dinner parties herself. Regina washes up. Pam is competent, drives the car – has done for years — is poised and mature. She loves Broome holidays and looking after her father. Greg is my sister's godfather, but he calls me 'godchild', which I like because he never talks down to me.

Rhoda Reynolds, Fred's favourite, is wearing sensational black taffeta shot with red lights; sadly for Fred, Jim Kennedy holds her hand. Beautiful Pat McDaniel is sophisticated in yellow chiffon; darkly attractive Peter Haynes, son of 'Doc' Haynes, our family doctor, and fair, irrepressible Terry McDaniel are popular with us all. There are many familiar faces, old childhood friends.

There are sixteen of us at the party, some home from Perth for holidays; others who stayed in Broome and have jobs already or go to school here and will journey south later to 'finish off'. We dance in a spacious room opening onto a latticed verandah, with the coconut matting rolled up. We waltz or foxtrot to shiny new 78 rpm records, holding one another romantically; 'You are My Lucky Star', 'I'm in Heaven', 'Please', 'Thanks for the Memory' are all favourites that year and played over and over again. The boys constantly wind up the gramophone by its metal handle, change records and screw new needles into the flexible silver arm.

Supper is sumptuous: cheese dreams; oysters in bacon; halved savoury eggs; sandwiches loaded with chopped prawns, crab, or grated Kraft cheese. Cream puffs, chocolate éclairs and meringues overflow with Nestlé's tinned cream; sponge rolls dribble strawberry jam. There are rich lamingtons and melting moments too. Jugs of fruit punch quench our thirst.

Helping ourselves from the buffet, refilling plates several

times, we sit or stand on the verandah, looking entranced at the bay's silver ripples and at the starry sky. The warm night air is full of smells – heavenly flower scents, briny whiffs of a full spring tide, the enticing aroma of juicy mangoes. A tradewind tosses palm fronds and ruffles our hair. Eyes strain towards William Dampier's Buccaneer Rock as we try to catch a glimpse of his ghost out there on the stony islet. Or better still, a sighting of Dampier's spectral frigate, the *Roebuck*, which still passes by at certain seasons, her gauzy sails filled by the tradewinds. The thought gives us excited goosebumps. Sometimes the guiding beacon built on a sand dune back from the water's edge, called the Ghost Light, mists over for no reason on clear nights. Legend says that when Will Dampier stands, cloaked and hatted, on the poop deck of his other-world ship, cruising from Buccaneer Rock and the bay, out to sea, the light mists over as he passes. My skin prickles whenever I see the blurred beacon. The Ghost Light is one of Broome's time-honoured mysteries and part of our folklore.

William Dampier, buccaneer, sea-rover and brigand, is Broome's fabled hero. He was the first Englishman to discover the pearling port, in 1688, when he beached his pirate barque, *Cygnet*, in a wide bay to repair the leaking vessel, look for fresh water and according to local legend, bury illicit treasure; men have been digging for the secret hoard ever since.

Dampier had a talent for popular writing and a passion for nature. On returning to England he published a journal describing strange seas and lands, which greatly impressed the British Admiralty. He was commissioned in 1699 to chart the

Southland's north-west coast and surrounding waters, in command of the frigate HMS *Roebuck*. He took the vessel into nameless seas in the southern hemisphere and returned to the wide bay. He overhauled his tall ship, explored the area and collected water before setting sail again. Two pieces of ancient cannon jettisoned in the harbour are still plain to see when the tide is out – they lie near Buccaneer Rock. When Dampier's journal was published, it inspired Jonathan Swift to write *Gulliver's Travels*. Dad says Swift placed Lilliput somewhere off the coast of Broome.

In memory of our explorer, Broome boasts a Dampier Terrace and Dampier Creek, and there's the Dampier Peninsula at Beagle Bay; further afield are the Dampier Archipelago in the south, and the Buccaneer Archipelago and Cygnet Bay near treacherous King Sound. His brave and enterprising spirit appeals to the trailblazers of the wild north-west.

We dance again until it's time to go home at eleven. Tom Peters, who's giving most of us a lift home, suggests boldly, 'Let's go to Cable Beach . . . the sides are up so no-one will fall off.' We know how rough and bouncy the tyre-track is, and Cable Beach at night, deserted, unlit, is out of bounds.

Nearly everyone shouts reckless agreement, carried away by the effect of dance music, balmy night, shining moon and first love. Having said our goodnights and thank yous to Mr and Mrs Reynolds, we climb, joking and laughing, onto the back of the truck. Fred and Edmund have found two attractive girls their age.

After a hair-raising jerky ride on the dirt track, Broome

behind us, Tom bumps to a stop at a clearing near the bluff at Cable Beach. We become couples lying on the tabletop under the stars, aware of the rhythmic thudding of waves and sighing backwash of restless currents on the beach below. The raw smell of the ocean is strong on the sea breeze. We recognise low intermittent sounds from night creatures in the scrubby bush: squeaks from a lone fruit bat, the whirr of a bird's wings, cheeping crickets, croaking frogs, rustling dry leaves as snakes and goannas hunt, muffled thumps as a lost joey hops. In the distance is the faint click of an Aborigine's clapsticks. Strangely, there are no plaguing mosquitoes or sandflies to bother us tonight.

Girls and boys gently embrace, kiss, murmur to one another. It's my first experience of what I imagine is 'making love', an exciting grown-up feeling. Gordon's arms around me, floating on a heavenly cloud in my green dress, faces together, he tenderly kisses my forehead, my lips. I kiss him softly back. It's bliss in the bright moonlight.

Mollie has chosen Nolan as her suitor; I wonder if they are as happy as we are. Soon, Tom says we'd better go, so cranking the engine, he leaps into the cabin, his girl by his side, and revs the motor. The truck lurches onto the red track again, heading for town and home.

Saying goodnight softly, we scramble from the truck. Realising that it's long past our expected homecoming, we stand in silence in the glare of moonlight. Edmund has gone his own way, so it's only Mollie, Fred and me. Knowing Dad will go off his brain if he's awake, we listen and hear the reassuring rumble of regular snores shaking the house. We creep silently up the shell path towards the front steps. Dad splutters, stops snoring; we stand rigid, silent as statues, even Fred. Scarcely breathing, we hope and wait for the snores to begin again. Soon they are louder than ever so we tiptoe quickly to our rooms, put on our pyjamas, and thankfully slide into our beds.

We are late waking in the morning. When we're up and dressed Mother tackles me sternly. 'Rosebud, you were very naughty staying out so late. You went to Cable Beach, didn't you? People are talking.'

Now I understand why the telephone kept ringing earlier, rousing me from deep sleep. 'Why are they talking?'

'It's not right for you youngsters to leave a party at eleven and come home well after midnight.'

'We only went to Cable Beach for a little while in Tom's tabletop.'

'That's the trouble, you're not supposed to be there at night and you know it.'

'But Mum, what's wrong? We only did some kissing and came home. Anyway, I'll be fifteen in April.' I laugh out loud, amazed at what Broome grown-ups think about. It's a shock.

In the evening, all forgiven, we take Mollie and Edmund to the Sun Open-Air Pictures in Carnarvon Street, a twice-a-week ritual we never miss.

Japtown looks quite different at night. The sun is setting on the horizon at faraway Cable Beach with its usual dramatic show, lighting the sky with flame reds and sunflower golds. With only a few streetlights, the town is transformed from brash corrugated iron into a dream world of glowing lights streaming from doorways. Contrasting inky shadows create uncanny optical illusions and I imagine that the alleyways of Broome must be just like those in Singapore and Shanghai, mixtures of haunting smells floating on the air and figures appearing and disappearing as they move swiftly in the hidden dark. We don't venture far from the Sun on picture nights, except to go to Ellies during the interval for their special lemon drinks.

Sun Pictures is run by Henry and Catherine Milner in partnership with Len Knight. They bring Hollywood to isolated Broome. Harry Milner also owns the ice and cordial factory with his elder son, Jim, handsome and charming as a film star. Milner senior runs the electricity station too.

The Sun Pictures building is half-roofed with iron. It is the centre of entertainment for Broome's multiracial community, opening on Wednesday and Saturday nights. Mr Milner and Mr Knight operate the enormous projectors; when a reel runs out we wait an interminable ten minutes while it is changed.

Mrs Milner makes the advertising dodgers by hand. Sometimes, when I'm visiting the Milner twins, Sheila and Flora, my friends since childhood, I lean eagerly over her deft handiwork. Information and drawings about a movie are laid out on a gelatine base sent up, with the films themselves, from Perth. Mrs M puts a clean sheet of coloured paper onto the shiny design, smoothes the paper with a wooden spatula and peels off the finished dodger. Gordon, the younger Milner son, delivers them to every household, then to the Japanese Club in town for collection. He speeds off on his bicycle, the sheets of vital information packed safely in a covered container.

The films are always well chosen for our mixed-race population. Nelson Eddy and Jeanette Macdonald sing their way into our hearts in costume romances; droll Eddie Cantor rolls his big brown eyes, singing and dancing with bevies of scantily dressed, even nude, Hollywood babes; suave Maurice Chevalier warbles his risqué French-accented songs, straw boater at an angle, jauntily swinging his cane, flirty eyes winking. Everybody's favourite is Charlie Chaplin, pathetic, funny and appealing. The Aborigines sitting on benches down the sides appreciate Chaplin's send-up of the white man in ridiculous clothes, bewildered movements, brilliant tragi-comedy. They fall off their seats laughing, and we laugh with them.

As you walk into the Sun, you see the seating layout, the roofed part sheltering cane armchairs in the centre for the white people, an aisle down the side separating more cane armchairs for top Chinese and Japanese citizens; everyone's comfortable seats are theirs permanently, as arranged with the Milners. In front of the reserved seats in the open under the stars are rows of deckchairs, not reserved but only for the whites if they want to sit there. Young children sit on benches in the front row under the screen. Aborigines and other Japanese, Chinese or Malays sit at the sides. Mother and Dad always sit in their cane chairs, but Fred and I prefer to sit with our friends in the deckchairs. Sometimes a cock-eye-bob blows up suddenly, the stars put out by black clouds, deafening thunder, streaks of cracking lightning and a blinding downpour of rain. All of us sitting in deckchairs in the open rush for cover and wait for the storm to pass just as quickly. Wet deckchairs don't stop us from sitting down again; in the heat they dry out in no time, while the picture continues once more.

We see all our friends on picture nights, and greet each other eagerly whatever our age. Sweet 'Koko' Forbes, most people's respected lawyer, is usually there. He has a gentle smiling face, well-brushed thick silver hair that curls around his ears and onto his white collar, and a warm soft voice. His mother was a member of the D'Oyly Carte family, producers of Gilbert and Sullivan's light operas. Nearly everyone in Broome owns the gramophone record of *The Mikado*, so the name of a favourite character, Koko, is given affectionately to Mr Forbes.

After we came back from England, I missed seeing Mrs Forbes and their four fine sons in Broome; Mrs F was one of my mother's best friends, a good-looking, educated woman. I learnt that she could see no future for her boys in the town's lean Depression years when everyone suffered economically, including her lawyer husband. She wanted her sons to have a good education and security, so she decided the only solution was to go back to Perth. Her husband had succumbed to

Broome's enchantment for men and he couldn't bear to leave. It was a sad story, but Mrs Forbes succeeded in seeing her sons well established in life, and remained close to my mother.

I asked my father where Koko lived now. 'On the foreshore,' he said airily, dismissing any further questions. There are many cultivated men living on the foreshore without their wives, including Uncle Mac. They are always immaculate in their white suits when they socialise. I can't imagine their wives tolerating living on the foreshore in dubious accommodation among the smelly mangroves, the grey mud, sandflies, mosquitoes and scuttling tiny red crabs, even though the view over Roebuck Bay is magnificent.

Topsy, our young Aboriginal maid, tells me spellbinding stories from her ancient Kimberley tribes when we are alone.

We are sitting at the wooden kitchen table polishing Mother's treasured brass. Tora is out of earshot; he considers he's from a higher order than other non-white races, especially the blacks. He never converses with them, only barks orders.

Dad has driven to his camp on the edge of town to rouse

the lethargic Malay crew who will be lolling in hammocks telling yarns, boasting of feminine conquests, gossiping about the latest snide pearl deal. As long as I can remember Dad has told us stories about pearls stolen at sea by a dodgy itinerant shell-opener, or a watchful deckhand, who, once in port, sells them on the snide market. There are furtive deals done in dark alleys. To stop the problem an owner or a trusted manager should be responsible for opening pearl-oysters, Dad says. Only the other day a big pearl pilfered at sea was rolling around in the back of Jimmy Chi's taxi, the thief having slunk ashore and lost it! The secret was out, everyone in Broome knew. The culprit could only lie low, his furious discomfort a source of amusement to the town.

I know what Dad will be shouting at the crew: 'What the hell are you lying down for, you blithering idiots? There's plenty to do on the luggers before we go to sea! You don't want to bloody drown; you want to come back for your girls, don't you?'

Today is another scorcher, no downpours lately to moisten the air, drench sun-baked red earth, fill water tanks. Cicadas strum ecstatically in the stillness. Black cockatoos streak across the sky, screaming raucously. From the timber mill in the bush opposite comes the discordant screeching of the circular saw. I'm frustrated and hot. Fred, Mollie and Edmund have fled to Cable Beach, and when Dad comes back with the car, Mother takes Daisy to Brownies. I am confined to barracks – or 'CB' – by my father for answering back. Soft cloth poised over a burnished tray, I sigh. 'A cock-eye-bob would make everything cooler,' I say. New green shorts and brief pink top cling damply to my skin. Topsy's flowered cotton shift skims her slight frame, revealing nothing. She lifts her dark head, fathomless eyes gaze past me.

'We make rain anytime. Wet, dry season all the same.'

'How, Topsy? Dry season, no can do,' I tease.

She's firm and points a slender finger eastwards to the limitless Kimberley pindan stretching far beyond Broome's settlement. 'The Rainmaker can make rain. I've seen it!'

I don't argue, knowing that it's true. Dad's told us many times of pulling in to Beagle Bay for fresh water when his fleet was fishing the pearling grounds off Cape Levêque, north of Broome. In the late nineteenth century, Roman Catholic priests journeyed from Germany and Italy to found the mission at Beagle Bay, with the intention of bringing spiritual enlightenment to the Aborigines. It's more than eighty miles by land from Broome, over pot-holed tyre-tracks across the pindan. Driving there in the 'Greengage' is a dusty half-day ordeal.

Once, when Dad's luggers arrived at the small peninsula, an Aboriginal lad from the mission ran onto the beach and called out for him to come and see the priest straightaway, as he was ill. Dad told the crew to fill the water tanks, then he walked up the track to mission headquarters, passing the tiny church made of local materials and built by the priests and Aborigines. Inside, the splendour of the chapel is amazing – shining mother-of-pearl everywhere, shell mosaics completely covering the altar in various patterns; they're replicas of Christian symbols combined with local Aboriginal tribal images.

Young Father Spendenberg was the priest in charge then. Dad knocked on the open door of his quarters, and Joseph, the boy who had called out to him earlier, padded to the entrance and beckoned him in. Dad walked into the spartan room and saw the priest lying on his rough bed. Greeting him, he asked if he had a fever. He took his temperature and felt his pulse – Dad studied medicine for a year before being lured by adventure to the South Seas. There didn't seem to be anything physically the matter, but Father Spendenberg was very worried about something. He finally told Dad of his deep concern.

He had directed the mission boys to start digging an irrigation channel from the well so that they could water some newly planted vegetable seedlings. Work was going ahead when the old Rainmaker appeared and told them to stop; there was no point carrying on as it was going to rain on Wednesday. In his own way he was either trying to help the situation, or attempting to prove that the old spells still worked. The boys stopped at once, in accordance with traditional belief. The priest was concerned for their spiritual wellbeing, and worried that without water the whole crop could be lost.

Of course Dad agreed that rain was out of the question in June; the wet season had finished in February and was over until November, and the glass showed fair weather. He told Father Spendenberg that when the promised rain failed to come on Wednesday, the boys would go back to digging, so not much time would be lost after all. But he felt for the young priest; far from home and support, his beliefs were challenged by ancient and powerful traditions.

Before leaving, Dad wanted to have a word with the Rain-maker, and asked Joseph to fetch him. An Aboriginal elder appeared from the bush; he was wearing rolled-up khaki trousers and a necklace of yellowing bones. Dad greeted the old man respectfully and explained that he shouldn't worry the new young Father by saying he could make rain in the dry season, and he should remember that before the priests came his people were always hungry, and now had beef, fresh vegetables, nets instead of spears to catch fish, and could read and write. The Rainmaker heard him out, smiling, then promised he would make rain on Wednesday, and with that disappeared into the scrub.

Dad's fleet sailed off into a glorious evening, a cloudless crimson-sunset sky, a smooth swell of darkening sea. The next day, Tuesday, was another perfect day, and they had good shell-gathering from dawn to dusk. On Wednesday morning Dad awoke to shouts from the crew. He climbed onto the deck and couldn't believe his eyes: a grey curtain of rain was heading across the sea towards the land and Beagle Bay. There was a heavy downpour for two hours, drenching luggers, the land and the vegetable garden at the mission. There had been no need for Father Spendenberg to worry about his crop. The rain cleared into fine weather, which lasted for the rest of the season.

Just before Christmas, Dad and the boys prepare for a promised lugger trip to look at iron-ore mining at Yampi Sound, an adventure the boys will never forget. Leases to mine the iron ore bordering the sound have just begun and Dad wants to watch what's going on. Dad and the boys say goodbye to us one afternoon, well loaded with sea-going gear, and drive off to the camp to prepare *Rosef* and the crew for the journey.

Fred comes back from the trip brimming with descriptions of the pristine coastal scenery, a scary swim, and how Dad's snores kept everyone awake at night, even echoing across the water to other boats in the area. He is careful to whisper this last piece of information when Dad is in another room; with Dad's volatility we can never be sure if he will join in the laughter, telling even more jokes at his own expense, or bawl us out for being cheeky. We make Fred start from the beginning; he describes how the lugger glided down Dampier Creek to Roebuck Bay, and on to the open sea. The following day she passed safely through reef-strewn waters and dropped anchor for the night before pressing on through the treacherous King Sound, a passage enclosed by islands on every side. He says that Koolan Island, the biggest of the group, is composed entirely of iron ore. They anchored in a canal ten miles long, went ashore and explored. Fred tells us how wild and beautiful the island is; waterfalls tumbling over cliffs into pools, one – 'Cleopatra's bath' – sparkling with crystal-clear water in a basin of gleaming quartzite, filling and flowing down into other pools. Rock wallabies bound up ledges to the summit.

After watching the mining at Koolan, Dad and the boys

sailed for Coppermine Creek to anchor for the night. Fred and Ed decided to go for a swim, and asked the crew if there were any sharks in the area. 'No,' they were assured, so the boys plunged in. 'No sharks; too many crocodiles!' They climbed quickly back onto the lugger! At dawn the following day, *Rosef* headed home.

We love hearing about the expedition, but do not envy the boys travelling in a cramped and heaving lugger in primitive conditions. It certainly wasn't a luxury cruise.

It is late afternoon, 24 December 1936, Christmas Eve. After a scorching day, the sun is heading for Cable Beach and will soon be a red ball sinking into the Indian Ocean, a signal for fruit bats living in the mangroves to go on the prowl as they flap silently across the pink sky.

We have been invited to the Secombes' for festive drinks: Gladys and Jack are our good friends, light-hearted, funny; they have two daughters – June, aged six, and Jackie, nine, Daisy's age. Jack runs a cattle station out of Broome, and owns a butcher shop in town. We walk down our winding shell path behind the house, past Dad's orchard of citrus, banana and mango trees, to the wrought-iron gate opening onto Guy Street and the hard, red-earth foot path. Seven of us – Mother, Dad, Daisy, Fred, Edmund, Mollie and I – talking amongst ourselves, pass the blacks' camp. The Aborigines are getting ready for tonight's corroboree, clapsticks click intermittently, smoke curls from fires cooking strange delicacies from the bush – animal and vegetable – and freshly caught fish from the jetty. The women are chattering excitedly, laughing children run about with their kangaroo-dogs, and the men are smearing themselves with white clay in symbolic patterns.

Almost opposite us and the camp is the Maguires' place; they are 'poor whites'. Mr Maguire drinks like a fish, we all know it. When he's in a drunken mood, loud screams are heard from the house; through the open latticed verandah we can't help seeing Mr Maguire chasing his wife, their six boys and girls of various ages running after them – round and round they go, vaulting over furniture, yelling at the tops of their voices. Thank goodness, the house is quiet this evening.

We walk past the old boab tree growing at the end of our street, its bottle-trunk swelling bulbously to the ground. It's a distorted goblin-tree out of Grimm's Fairy Tales. You can live inside an ancient hollow boab. Many people have, like in the giant tree outside Derby that's thirty feet in diameter. The Hillgrove Boab at Wyndham was once lock-up for up to thirty native prisoners chained inside it. The swollen trunk can store large amounts of fluid and no two trees are alike, differing in size and shape, but looking unmistakably a boab. The skeletal branches claw upwards to the sky, resembling a spidery root system; the Aborigines say in their folklore it's an upside-down tree.

In the wet season the bare branches sprout broad green leaves, a haven for nesting birds; large buds also form, opening at night into creamy-coloured flowers which develop into big, brown, fuzzy-shelled fruit that stay on the branches when the leaves drop. As a little girl, I've broken the husks with my friends the Milner twins, and eaten the pulpy white flesh inside – it's not appetising, tasting acidic and salty.

Turning the corner we are at the Secombes' gate, and Gladys and Jack greet us warmly. The house is full, guests spill onto the verandahs and into the garden, or sit in the spacious living room that leads onto encircling wide latticed areas. Most of the men are outside, clutching refreshing glasses. They're dressed in starched white cotton suits; the women wear smart cool frocks. Loud happy voices, ripples of laughter, send soundwaves of good cheer into the still air.

We smell the pleasant aroma of burning insect coils keeping bloodthirsty mosquitoes at bay. We put our torches on a table near the door; walking home in the dark without them is dangerous, it's easy to tread on a reptile or a scorpion. One night Mother and I nearly stepped on a tangle of thin whip snakes entwined like silvery Chinese noodles.

Tilly, the Secombes' Aboriginal maid, circulates with a tray of fresh lemon squash in icy glasses for the young people. Adults help themselves from the drinks table. Bowls of salted nuts and plates of delicious savouries are enticing. In the living room the grown-ups are planning a party – there is time spare for social life during the long lay-up season. Gladys is enthusi-astic. 'We'll have a dress-up Book Title party – Jack can leave the bottom button of his fly undone and go as *Disgrace Abound-ing*!' Everyone in Broome is reading the Douglas Reed book. I laugh, pretty daring of him! Someone else asks for clues on how to go as *Eyeless in Gaza* by Aldous Huxley.

Mollie and I move out to the verandah where purple bougainvillea drops petals onto floorboards. Our brothers and friends are standing in groups . . . Pam Gregory, the McDaniels, Shirley Ogilvie, the crowd. Pat McDaniel is reminding us about tomorrow, Christmas Day: after present opening and early church, we'll drive with our parents to Cable Beach for our traditional swim and choruses of 'Happy Christ-mas' to one another. Refreshed, there's a bumpy drive home; the rest of the day is devoted to preparing and consuming the Christmas feast at Broome's hottest time of the year. We cling to our forebears' time-honoured customs in wintry Britain. Asian houseboys and coloured maids help the Missus cook the mad white man's tucker – hot roast poultry, fresh vegetables, jugs of gravy, a leg of ham and all the trimmings. A tinned plum pudding brought out from the storeroom and opened, filled with sterilised silver sixpences and trinkets knifed in by Mother, heated, set alight on a serving dish and carried flaming to the table. Mother cuts steaming wedges onto plates. We help our-selves to Nestlé's tinned cream.

Walking away for a moment to look more closely at a flow-ering frangipani tree growing against the verandah rail, I'm suddenly grabbed around the waist from behind, a muscular hand firmly cups one of my small breasts and I'm swung around by Captain K, a white-haired family friend, a pearler and now, I realise, a lecher. His head swoops down as he plants his predatory mouth on mine in a crushing kiss. Outraged, flushing scarlet, assaulted, I break away; running, I find Mother and hiss the episode into her ear. She smiles casually and pats my hand: 'Never mind, darling, he does it to everyone.' Shocked, a flash of enlightenment strikes too. The kiss would not have been so disturbing if the kisser had been young, handsome Edmund. I would have swooned in ecstasy! Nothing so explicitly physical has happened before; when Gordon and I kissed each other, it was chaste and sweet, not repellent.

Striving for a nonchalant demeanour, hoping the hot, flustered feeling will disappear quickly, I talk sternly to myself . . . Forget what happened. Pat, Shirley, Pam, even Mollie, would probably have taken the incident in their stride, would have kicked the old pig in the crotch – as we've been cautioned – and walked away laughing. Blast my naïve outlook! Four years of heaven in England, protected from all unpleasantness, ignorant and innocent . . . Back in Australia three years ago, straight to boarding school in Perth, cooped up with other girls, we're always talking about boys. Some have a little knowledge of males; Hetty is believed to have 'done it', although she hasn't told us what it's like. Deciding to erase all memory of the silly kiss, I stroll down the side steps to the darkening, crowded garden before rejoining my chums, still cavorting and in stitches.

I pass a circle of pearlers, including my father, in animated conversation. I can't help overhearing some of it. They discuss the Japanese who fish illegally for pearl-shell off north-west Australia during our lay-up; Broome pearlers would not risk their crew members' lives during the monsoon season. Dad calls them fatalistic devils; they seem to accept drowning in cyclones. They have a strong belief in the afterlife: 'If today is my day to die, I die.'

'Look at our coastline, my friends, our waters, deserted, empty during monsoon time when the bloody pirates creep in on the sly . . . Government should send a warship here once a year to scare them off . . .'

I've heard this kind of talk many times. There are worries about teeming Asia having its eyes on Australia.

Calm now, I hasten to be with my pals, forget about the Japanese raiders and Captain K. The weeks after Christmas will fly, and we'll be on the boat again, back to school, and I won't see my mother for a year.

Part II

Early Years, to 1929

The old photograph album has been closed for a long time. It belonged to my father, Louis Goldie, and now after many years I open the fat book once more.

Memories surface as I look at the photos: Dad taking his album from a drawer, the ritual repeated each year while we were home in Broome from boarding school for the Christmas holidays. There is enjoyment and curiosity for youthful eyes taking in foreign places, strange people, significant moments captured in black and white. As we cluster around him, Dad, clearly wistful, recalls his irrepressible youth while explaining each photo, where it was taken, an individual's identity.

Now as I turn the dark green cardboard pages, fragile, split and brown at the edges, I'm surprised to find the photos still quite clear, although the writing underneath has faded. Most pictures record Dad's carefree days in the Torres Strait Islands and Dutch East Indies early in the twentieth century.

On one page I gaze at European master pearler and millionaire, Louis Moreau, on a festival day in Makassar. He is surrounded by family and a crowd of employees. It's 1911. My father was a young apprentice commanding some of Mr Moreau's pearling boats while learning about the business.

I puzzle again over the mystery photograph on a page by itself – the exotic Asian beauty in a traditional sarong, a splendid necklace around her throat, posing formally on high cushions. Was she the daughter of the Javanese grandee who promised my father untold wealth if he married her? Dad would never tell us the seductive maiden's name, although we had often heard the story of the rich man's offer. Now I'm sure she was the tycoon's daughter! Mother's expression was always enigmatic when this photo was discussed.

A few personal snaps are included: my father in 1901, aged fifteen, wears a Sydney Grammar straw boater. Seven years on he has left home with high hopes; here are the reef-strewn waters of the Torres Strait and across the sea in the distance is Booby Island. Happy scenes on Thursday and Prince of Wales islands follow.

A tiny snap, a historical record of Lord Kitchener's arrival at Thursday Island, then known as the Shire of Torres, on Christmas Day 1908, is still sharp and clear after all these years. Clad in white, Kitchener is unmistakable with his bushy moustache as he inspects a uniformed guard of honour presenting arms.

A graceful schooner, *Wanetta*, fully rigged, skims a light swell in 1910; she's a famous beauty in these parts.

Amongst all the memorabilia are records of young men formally grouped, Dad among them, holding rifles, dressed in khaki uniforms, cocked hats on their heads, 1910; the same male gathering in tropical whites parties around a white-draped table, champagne bottles in the foreground, weapons stacked behind them. These are pictures of Thursday Island's Rifle Club, a testament to that outpost of the Empire and loyalty to the Crown.

Dad arrived in Broome early in 1912. An enlarged early photograph of Broome's frontier settlement tells the story of its lonely habitation. Called Japtown then and Chinatown after World War II, when all things Japanese were anathema, it was a motley collection of wooden and corrugated-iron buildings huddled together, low and unadorned. The small town sat above the mangrove foreshores of Roebuck Bay; a wide earth road strewn with broken shells ran through it, a high cloudless sky stretched overhead.

A would-be Kimberley grazier, W. F. 'Bill' Tays, was instrumental in founding the Broome pearling industry. While walking along a beach at Nickol Bay near Roebourne in 1866, he saw Aborigines wearing nothing but large, silvery pearl-shells. Impressed, he coaxed them into collecting the shell at low tide when the oyster beds were exposed. It was soon clear to him that pearl-shell sales were far more profitable than sending sheep to market. Tays's success attracted other failed pastoralists and the news spread. It was the Gold Rush all over again, but unlike gold, which had been exhausted after only four years at Halls Creek in the Kimberley, there seemed to be plenty of pearl-shell for everyone.

The worldwide demand from the button trade and from craftsmen for the largest and purest mother-of-pearl shells made men rich in a very short time. And if you were lucky, you'd find a beautiful pearl and an even richer reward in an opened oyster.

Broome was close to the biggest colonies of pearl-shell, a natural destination for pearl-seekers to establish themselves.

The laying of submarine telegraph cable by the British Australian Telegraph Company between Broome and Java in 1889 linked this outpost to the rest of the world.

The settlement lies on a flame-red peninsula jutting out into the sparkling sapphire Indian Ocean, whose tides race into Roebuck Bay and surge over grey mud through mangrove thickets to become flowing creeks and tapering foreshore streams. Within a few hours, magnetic forces pull the sea back again and the creeks are emptied, turquoise water recedes from the bay and out to the horizon and the ocean is a blue band in the distance. Twice-yearly at equinox, the king tides rise and fall thirty feet, flooding parts of the town.

Broome's bay and creeks are natural havens for sailing craft and crew camps. Before immigration restrictions in 1901, men from the different Asian countries flocked to the developing town, bringing their women, Eastern spices, vaporous incense, jangling music, foreign languages, exotic religious rituals, and glowing paper lanterns to light up crooked lanes and alleys at night before electricity came to the settlement. Local Aborigines crowded in to see what was going on, made their camps, mingled with the townsfolk, and before long there evolved a hybrid people of tangled blood-lines.

Broome rapidly became the bustling pearling hub of the north-west, experiencing a golden age for pearl-fishing in the early years of the twentieth century. Up to four hundred luggers were packed into Roebuck Bay at lay-up time, and more than three thousand Asians lived in ramshackle Japtown.

The remoteness of our settlement strikes one immediately

and vividly. Vast dune fields of the Great Sandy Desert – gibber gibber country – meet the immense ruby-red Kimberley wilderness at Halls Creek. The Kimberley claims the pearl coast at Broome before rolling north-east to Wyndham. Kimberley men were trailblazers – cattle kings and pearling masters with a devil-may-care attitude and a taste for adventure. Kimberley women were their loyal mainstays – courageous and determined, they created secluded homesteads in the wilderness. There were nautical homes set up by wives on pearling luggers in the old days, too, though none remained when I was growing up. Indeed, by then, an unwritten law decreed that white women were not permitted to stay overnight on a lugger.

Shaking off reveries, more photographs beckon: two coastal steamers with tall funnels, typical of the era, are on either side of the half-mile-long jetty, sitting high and dry, the swift tide not yet returned to claim them. Back in town there are some tiny verandahed cottages near Japtown, shutters propped open, sea-shell paths neatly edged with amber-coloured upturned beer bottles sunk level with the ground.

There's a snap of Dad's camp, roughly thatched tin sheds, where crew and carpenters work and live while on land; some luggers nearby are in shallow trenches along the mangroves waiting for repairs. Dad sits for the shot on an upturned dinghy, dapper in formal whites, bow tie, polished dark shoes. Some thirty Asian crewmen group around him, standing or squatting in casual shirts, baggy trousers. Dad looks right at home, completely at ease with his men and his surroundings.

I often think of the strange and fateful story of how my

father came to Broome in 1912 and became a pearler, and a few years later brought my elegant English mother to live in one of the most isolated and rudimentary towns in the Western world.

My father was born Louis Isaac Goldstein in Melbourne on 5 May 1886, the eldest of four children. The family was Jewish, their name originally Sandrich, I was told. Escaping persecution in Poland for the relative safety of England, an ancestor changed his surname to Goldstein, the name of the benefactor who sheltered him there. My grandfather, Aaron, emigrated from England to Melbourne and became an Australian citizen. He soon distinguished himself in rowing, winning two silver medals for the state of Victoria in 1876. Aaron was a respected gem merchant with coppery-coloured hair and, it is said, a mercurial temper. He would pass both these characteristics on to his eldest son. Aaron married my grandmother, Fanny Vince, a Jew of Dutch descent, in 1885. She was quite different from him, with curly black hair, deep blue eyes 'put in with a smudged finger', as the saying went, and a firm but loving nature.

I have a studio photograph of Dad and his siblings. They're good-looking, posed in their best clothes on a fur-covered sofa. My father looks 'trendy' according to his great-grandchildren, wearing rimless small round glasses, broad white collar, floppy black bow tie, fitted dark suit, calf-length tightly laced polished boots and a quizzical smile. His sisters, Daisy especially, are pretty, with long curly hair brushing their shoulders, and the youngest in the family, Percy, is dark and appealing.

While the children were still young, Aaron moved his family to a house in the harbourside suburb of Darling Point, Sydney, and bought a site at 189 Pitt Street in the city, from which to launch a jewellery shop: The Modern Art Jewellery Company. It was later sold to Mr William Proud, who developed the business into today's multi-store undertaking.

As strictly Orthodox Jews (my grandfather was descended from a rabbinical dynasty), my grandparents observed Jewish rites and traditions throughout the year. Kosher food was served in the household. Mixing meat with dairy products was banned, and many other dietary rules were adhered to. The daily rituals and the chanting and reading of the sacred Torah in the synagogue on the Sabbath permeated my father's soul and every fibre of his being. At thirteen, he celebrated his bar mitzvah, the solemn rite of passage from boyhood to manhood.

Dad's family was intensely loyal to Australia and to the Mother Country, and Dad had a conventional upbringing. He was educated at Sydney Grammar School and went on to study medicine at the University of Sydney. He was an ebullient redhead, intelligent and gregarious. He liked the student life, but perhaps too much; he failed his first-year exams. Gold-stein senior was furious and refused to waste any more money on university fees, insisting instead that Louis join him in the family business. Bitterly disappointed, Louis announced that he'd prefer to follow the pearl rush to Broome. His idea was to put up his shingle in Broome as an expert pearl-cleaner, earn enough money to buy a lugger and in time build up his own fleet.

By the beginning of the twentieth century news had spread all over the world of fortunes being made from the newly discovered pearling grounds in Australia's north-west. Crystal-clear seas were responsible for the huge mother-of-pearl shells' healthy growth and unblemished moon-silver nacre, which also produced pearls of perfect lustre and of a quality rarely found elsewhere. Having spent holidays in his father's workroom, Dad knew a lot about gems and had experience cleaning pearls. Indeed, he had been brought up to have a passion for pearls. Aaron was a world expert on them, and had even journeyed to Russia in 1907 to view *La Pellegrina*, or the 'Queen of Pearls', then on display in a Moscow museum. This pearl was said to have a spellbinding effect on all who saw it, a reputation that drew lovers of these precious natural wonders to gaze on the miracle of its beauty. Though there remains some confusion between it and another famous pearl, *La Peregrina*, it allegedly passed through many famous hands: King Philip II is said to have given it to the Tudor queen of England, Mary, upon their marriage in 1554. It remained in England until Charles II sold it to France. Later, it is thought to have belonged to a Russian princess and Prince Louis Napoleon of France, and in more recent times, it is said, to Elizabeth Taylor, a present from her then husband, Richard Burton.

My father always carried with him the memory of Aaron's rapturous description of the pearl on his return: 'It's the loveliest pearl in the world, a perfect sphere of matchless colour, lustre and skin; certainly the one and only queen of pearls.'

Resigned to his son's departure from Sydney, Aaron eventually arranged an apprenticeship with an old friend, millionaire pearler Louis Moreau, whose fleet was based in the Dutch East Indies. My father often told us that his years there, and on Thursday Island, were some of the happiest of his life. Then, ready to fulfil his dream of starting out on his own, my father stepped ashore onto Broome's long jetty in early 1912 and fell in love with the place. He always said that home is where you hang your hat, and Broome was where he hung his.

Broome was still basking in its heyday in 1912, a boom town on the make. It grew along the mangrove-lined shores of Roebuck Bay, a jumble of buildings, some two-storeyed, the narrow lanes and boardwalks crowded with different races; most of them there to cash in on the pearl-shell industry in any way they could. There were pubs, billiard saloons, international pearl-buyers' offices (Mark Ruben reputedly the most successful of all), general stores owned by pearlers Robison & Norman and Streeter & Male, a Chinese tailor and two Chinese drapers, a Japanese tombstone carver, C. E. Heinke & Co.'s showroom, displaying the latest diving equipment manufactured in England, cafes and a special restaurant for the Japanese, banks, boarding houses, gambling dens, brothels, outside iron WCs inevitably surrounded by angry blowflies, and a Chinese *dhobi*, or laundry, where the pearlers' white suits were washed and ironed, the irons heated by charcoal. There was everything to satisfy the diverse population.

In Dampier Creek, luggers were drawn up on the foreshore, resting in trenches beside pearlers' camps. The master pearlers who were making big money owned graceful supply schooners, mother ships to service their fleets at sea. Vessels were refitted and reconditioned at foreshore camps during lay-up from November to March, and in the dry they returned at intervals laden with pearl-shell to be unloaded and sorted in shell sheds. Sometimes they sailed back with a dead diver on board; many died from the bends before they could reach Broome and its decompression chamber, which arrived in 1914, others drowned and some were never found.

On the outskirts of town, married pearlers were building pretty, latticed bungalows to suit the climate. Gardens were planted; underground water – plentiful, but hard, brown and metallic-smelling – was brought in from an artesian bore in those days before spring water was found; rainwater was conserved for drinking. Some pearlers and their wives still lived either on a lugger or a schooner, their children too.

Dad met other young men with similar interests and soon they became good friends. Many were working on luggers for established pearlers – legendary tycoons such as James Clarke and Mark Ruben. Some were in partnership with friends, or were building up their own fleets: men like Ted Norman, whose father was a pioneer of Broome's pearling industry, brothers Ancell and Dick Gregory, Beresford and Bernard Bardwell, Syd Pryor, Claude Hawkes, Harry MacNee, Mac McDaniel, Fred Everett, Mac Mackenzie and Morrie Lyons. They were a happy band of good companions who lived by the rules of mateship; there was surprisingly little rivalry.

There were a few women in Broome, too, including the wives of older, established pearlers, like tall and beautiful Phyllis Bardwell of Sydney, artist and sister of the Bardwell brothers, who married dashing Mac McDaniel. Adventurous girls arrived in the settlement to work as barmaids. Understanding, bright and good-looking, some took second careers as mistresses to the men who were starved of female company. Those who didn't mind the heat, isolation, the biting insects and ever-present snakes married lonely pearlers, settled in pleasant bungalows, were loyal wives and good mothers. Some master pearlers' wives came from conservative families down south or from the eastern states, and some of them refused to meet ex-barmaids at afternoon tea parties or at the card table. It was a very rough and unfamiliar world for them; many left. But usually their husbands stayed on.

Always gregarious, a man's man to the core, Dad was in his element in male-dominated Broome. He never comprehended the female sex, although he grew up with two younger sisters. (He never asked Mother her opinion on anything; she gave it anyway.) Women had to be pretty, feminine, even flirtatious to gain his attention, but he was happiest in the company of other men. There is early proof of Dad's ambivalence towards females when, at eighteen, he wrote a popular comic verse in his sister Daisy's autograph album:

A woman is a stubborn thing
And hard to manage till —
You learn that when she will, she won't,
And when she won't she will.

I have often wondered if my father's attitude to women was an example of traditional pioneer Aussie mateship, or if it stemmed from the significance of maleness in his Jewish background. Women were so often segregated, seated apart from the men in the synagogue, and at *minyan*, a Friday evening prayer meeting that had to comprise of no fewer than ten men – women, by law, could not make up the head count in those days.

Not all white males in Broome were interested in pearling. They made other contributions essential to the growing hamlet. In addition there were a few Englishmen with aristocratic backgrounds, charming 'remittance men', who were paid by their families to live as far from home as possible, having caused scandals in the old country.

My father's first year in Broome was eventful. Though my friends and I were born years later, we all knew about the sinking of the *Koombana* out of Port Hedland in a willy-willy on 22 March 1912; the pearl-buyer Mr Abraham E. Davis was on board, brother-in-law and business partner of Mark Ruben. Local legend says he'd just bought a fabulous pearl, the Roseate Pearl, a bringer of bad luck; dark deeds, infamous murders and subsequent hangings accompanied the pearl's reputation. Davis bought it from a desperate seller just before the *Koombana* sailed, but the priceless pearl ended up on the bottom of the sea whence it came. This was not the end of the story; Davis had lived in the prettiest bungalow in Broome. It was large with graceful lines; elaborate white fretwork surrounded the latticed verandahs. It was later acquired by the Anglican Church and was called the Bishop's Palace. Anglican bishops of the vast north-west lived there when in Broome. But Davis's ghost had been seen gliding in and out of his former home by many people. One bishop who'd seen it had attempted to lay the restless spirit. He may have been successful, but we all loved the spooky story of the hauntings. We thought Davis may have been looking for another lost pearl.

Dad established himself, found office premises and had a white sign made upon which appeared, hand-printed in black writing: 'L. I. Goldstein Pearl Cleaner'. (It is now in the Broome Museum.) He still dreamed of buying a small fleet of his own, and often browsed through the showroom of the much-respected C. E. Heinke & Co., which had supplied the equipment to the master pearlers Dad had worked for before arriving in Broome, and was the best-known supplier of diving equipment to Japan, the Dutch East Indies, Thursday Island and northern Australia. Dad would often talk to the showroom's manager, Mr Ogilvie, about the equipment: hand-pumps and diving 'dresses', rubber hoses and huge diving helmets. He was not to know how fateful this connection would be.

Dad lived with friends in a boarding house and joined the rifle club as he had in Thursday Island so he'd be ready to fight and defend the Mother Country if war came. And it did, in 1914. In September of that year, Dad sailed to Fremantle in the *Charon,* and the day after landing enlisted in the AIF's 16th Battalion at Blackboy Hill Camp. After a spell in Melbourne at Broadmeadows Camp, the battalion was sent to Egypt in the *Berrima* with the first reinforcements in February 1915. The 16th served at Heliopolis until they were sent to Gallipoli. Dad landed at Anzac Cove at 6 am on 25 April 1915, a date that has become an integral part of Australian history and folklore. He fought in filthy trenches alongside his Broome friend, Harry MacNee, who famously caught the Turks' grenades in his hands like cricket balls, throwing them back again like a true Test fielder, but with a deadlier purpose. Dad was badly wounded at Pope's Hill – he never told us how – but later rejoined his battalion at Aghyl Dere, and served there until the evacuation. He went on to Egypt until June 1916, when the troopship *Canada* took his battalion to Europe. There he fought in the trenches of France and Belgium, and was

Dad in his officer's uniform.
He served in the 16th Battalion AIF in World War I.

wounded for a second time at Mouet Farm, France. Nevertheless, upon recovery he was posted to La Douve River, Belgium, where he was injured a third time, and finally returned to fight in France until the end of the war. He later told us amusing stories of his wartime experiences, but he never mentioned that he had been buried for twelve hours in one bomb blast, which had crushed his chest. Mother told me about this years later.

Dad had a scar like a deep fold of skin running diagonally down his back from shoulder to waist, the result of an injury which had been termed a 'broken back'. I saw the scar many times but seldom thought twice about it as a child; now I realise the horror it represented. Dad would take bore-water baths to ease the pain the wound still caused; he never fully recovered from the assaults on his body and mind. In between his many wartime sorties, while recovering in England, he met my mother.

Catherine Doris Sprang, usually called Do or Dodo, was born on 24 January 1891, the second daughter of Catherine and

Frederick Sprang. Their firstborn, Lily, died of pneumonia, aged nine, leaving Mother the eldest. She and her younger brother, Billy, and sisters Gay and Joy, enjoyed an idyllic childhood. Her parents adored each other and their children. There were servants, nannies, gentle discipline; everything in my mother's world was ordered, protected, joyous. She took for granted the soft greens of England, the wildflowers, musical bird calls, the four seasons bringing distinct changes to her world. She loved the history and heritage of her country, its ancient buildings and charming villages.

In their teenage years Mother and her younger sister Gay were sent to a girls' boarding school, Queenswood, where they learnt conventional subjects along with other skills such as deportment, how to enter and leave a carriage – automobiles were only just appearing – and all the other accomplishments expected of a young lady.

When Mother left school she went to dances, parties, the theatre. She helped her mother host the many church fetes held in the big garden at their home in Bromley. There were visits to Paris, too; Mother spoke fluent French.

Mother had been a tomboy when growing up, her clothes always in a mess, but she blossomed into an exceptionally beautiful woman with great charm, vivacity, intelligence and a positive outgoing nature. She also had spirit and a strong character, and was blessed with a fine mezzo-soprano voice. My grandparents sent her to London's Royal Academy of Dramatic Art for singing lessons, elocution and to learn the violin. She would sing and recite poetry at charity concerts and drawing-room gatherings, and recalled to me that her mother used to give her a posy of scented violets to wear on these occasions. It was never intended that she become a professional; it was standard for young women with these talents to receive this sort of training.

I think of my mother as a storybook princess, 'as good as she was beautiful', her skin flawless white, hair black and curly, fine arched eyebrows, even white teeth, a curved smiling mouth, her big eyes a compelling colour, sometimes blue, sometimes mossy green, changing according to her clothes, mood, health. She was of medium height, slim, and attracted people to her side like a magnet.

There were many suitors; on one occasion my grandmother took her daughters to Switzerland to enjoy the winter sports, and a persistent young baron, heir to a fortune and staying at the same chateau, asked for Mother's hand in marriage. Nineteen-year-old Doris, however, wasn't interested.

With the coming of the Great War in 1914, Mother's younger brother, Billy, joined the army as an officer and my mother began voluntary work in a London hospital as a nurses' aide. Sometime in late 1915 or early 1916 my grandfather told his family that a young Australian soldier would be visiting them. My mother learnt that he'd been living in Broome, had interests in pearls and in pearl-shell diving, and had contacted her father at his factory in Bermondsey.

This was not the first time Australians from Broome had been entertained by the Sprangs. Mr Sprang befriended servicemen from pearling colonies, notably my father's friend and master

An original C. E. Heinke diving helmet,
photographed in the window of Paspaly's Darwin jewellery shop.

pearler Dick Gregory, younger brother of Ancell, who with his pregnant wife, Alice, had arrived in England earlier, but sadly was killed in the Middle East. The Australian this time was my father, wearing his officer's uniform. Before leaving Broome, he had asked Mr Ogilvie at C. E. Heinke & Co. for an introduction to the firm's chairman, Fred Sprang, in the event that during the uncertainties of war he found himself in England. He arrived at the Sprang home with his brother, Percy, also in uniform, but with one leg missing thanks to the action he'd seen in France. The brothers had been reunited in England. My mother and her sisters were waiting to help entertain the young men.

There was an instant attraction between my parents. Doris thought Louis was full of fun, informal but polite, good-looking in an unusual way with his red hair and green eyes. Percy was quite different: tall, so handsome you had to look twice, with jet-black hair and a steady gaze. He was charming in a quiet, reserved way – but it was my father Mother was drawn to. For his part Dad could hardly believe he'd met this stunning woman, and she was powerful Fred Sprang's heiress daughter! It was love at first sight. My father began to court her at once and soon asked my grandfather for her hand. There is no doubt that they were both deeply in love.

However, they faced a difficult and painful path. Anti-Semitic feeling ran deep in England, and as a condition of marriage my grandfather insisted that my father change his name and religion – and promise never to take my mother to Broome. The backgrounds and upbringing of the two were entirely different. How could such a cultured gentlewoman survive in Broome? my grandparents argued. Having been there himself, my grandfather knew its isolation and feared his daughter would not cope. Mother told me that her suitor was lyrical about the place, however, as all men were when describing it to her. She was captivated by the idea of adventure, of breaking out of her mould, and yearned to try a different life. My father was so determined to marry her he had no hesitation in becoming a Christian, changing his middle name from Isaac to John and his surname from Goldstein to Goldie (which he chose because it was his nickname among the Broome pearlers). Finally, although my grandfather got down on his knees and begged my mother to end her relationship with Dad, they were married on 29 November 1916 at Rompell Park Church in the district of Lambeth, county of London, while Dad was on leave from fighting in France.

When he heard the full story, Dad's father, Aaron, disowned his eldest child, holding a burial ceremony, complete with empty coffin, in the Sydney synagogue. He forbade his wife and children ever to speak to my father again, believing that to renounce one's Judaism was akin to ceasing to exist. Percy and Daisy, however, privately never lost touch.

I understand now that something died within Dad when he heard his father's decision, and afterwards I don't think he ever really knew who he was. Although he accepted and believed in Christianity – he made sure we all knew he'd given up cigarettes for Lent! – I discovered later that he always gave quiet support to Broome's Jewish community, especially when someone died. Many years later when I met his sister Daisy, she fondly remembered with a smile the old days before Dad left Sydney: 'Wherever Louis was there was always fun and laughter.'

My brother Fred was born on 8 July 1918, and the war ended a few months later. In 1919, when Fred was a year old, Dad insisted on going back to the life he knew instead of accepting an offer by my grandparents to set him up with his own pearl-buying business in London. My grandparents had serious misgivings, but my mother was willing and adventurous, and although she was again pregnant, she and her bonny baby son sailed with Dad in the *Orsova* on the long journey to Fremantle. Her parents were heartbroken, already devastated by the loss of their beloved son, Billy, who had been killed in the trenches of France. Not long before the ship docked in Western Australia, Mother suffered an advanced miscarriage, a little boy she later told me, and was carried off the ship when it arrived in port. She underwent a curette in a Perth hospital before boarding another vessel for Broome, to begin a strange and tumultuous life she could never have imagined. It was a lifestyle, though, that forged her into a strong and unforgettable woman, a true pioneer of early Broome, who was admired and greatly loved by all who knew her.

For his part, Dad returned to Broome a changed man from the Louis Goldstein who had left five years earlier. He'd survived the war and now had a beautiful, cultured and wealthy wife, a powerful father-in-law, a baby son and an English nanny, supplied and paid for by my grandmother, to complete his entourage. The family stayed at first in the Continental Hotel, which was rudimentary but the best in Broome, and would soon build one of the largest and prettiest bungalows in the town (now one of the few originals left). My father felt he had fallen squarely on his feet and intended to make a success of his life.

I was born in our Broome house at sunrise on 1 April 1922. The birds were singing and I was in a hurry to enter the world, a month early; my mother used to say with a laugh, 'Making your mother an April fool!' My brother Fred was four. My elder sister, Dolly, had died two years before, a frail baby who had lived only four months. In those days few lifesaving infant formulas were available and there was no quick way to deliver to Broome the only one that the local doctor thought could have been suitable.

Dolly is buried in the hard red earth of the white section of the Broome cemetery, her christening name, Doris Catherine Fanny, engraved on a baby-size white marble scroll. A huge beautiful conch shell lies beside the grave, a permanent offering. (I was never taken there, but went to the site years later when visiting Broome. I cried and tried to tear out the weeds, replacing them with the only wildflowers growing in the starkness.)

Her death broke my mother's heart. She said Dolly's big blue eyes used to follow her everywhere from the cradle. Mother told me that when she awoke on the morning after Dolly's death, she had a strong vision of her adored late brother Billy carrying her baby in his arms, surrounded by light; the experience comforted her.

Fred remembered Dolly – indeed 'Dolly' was his name for her as he couldn't pronounce 'Doris'. The grief in the house, the isolation, the lack of specialist health care and suffocating heat were all too much; Fred became a thin, nervous child after being a bubbly and robust toddler. He had been born in a private hospital in England under the best specialist care, with an obstetrician, maternity sisters and nurses in attendance. In contrast, Mother's three daughters were born in her bed at home. A Perth midwife, Nurse Grover, sailed up to Broome to attend each birth and stayed for a month afterwards, and when labour began a trained nun from the St John of God convent also attended. 'Doc' Haynes, the local GP, delivered each baby.

Fortunately, Nurse Grover had arrived by the time Mother went into labour with me. Mother and Dad used to say with relief, 'You were a strong baby, like a plump puppy.' Every week I put on the exact weight according to the book.

Fred and I were a pigeon pair, and my delighted father named his latest lugger *Rosef* after us. My brother and I looked alike in many ways. He had fair skin, blue eyes, golden curls and a happy laughing nature. My skin was even fairer – harsh sunlight made it a mass of powdery freckles, which I hated. My eyes were hazel; my hair rust-red curls inherited from Dad. I had a happy nature too, except when thwarted – then I screamed.

I was named Rosemary in remembrance of Dolly, but Dad insisted on his daughters being given Catherine as their first name (except for Dolly, whose second name it was) after our maternal grandmother, Catherine Sprang, who had been kind and understanding during the dispute over his marriage to Mother, trying to work with the situation rather than cause further problems. We were to be called by our middle names and I forgot about my 'Catherine' until the computer age, when it appeared on all my files.

My nanny was a big Aboriginal woman called Black Elsie – an affectionate nickname and not at all offensive back then. (Fred's English nanny, dazzled by the attention in female-starved Broome, had left our house in scandalous circumstances when my parents arrived home one night to find two men fighting over her in the living room.) We had a photograph of Elsie holding me, and I loved her. My parents had shortened

Rosemary to Rosebud, and Elsie took it a step further to Buddy, which remained my Broome name from that time on. Sadly, Elsie left us when I was very young and I never saw her again.

Also ever-present in our household was Tora, our Japanese cook and houseboy, who had come to work for my parents when they moved into their new bungalow.

An Aries, I was always ahead of myself. I was impatient with my dummy and always 'spat' it, and my first word was 'pretty'. Years later when I read the Bible and found, 'Whatsoever things are true . . . whatsoever things are lovely, if there be any praise, think on these things . . .' in Philippians, the advice resonated deeply within me and still does.

I was a pest to my poor brother, who enjoyed playing peacefully with his toys on the side verandah. When I became mobile and was put down on the opposite verandah I'd inch determinedly on my bottom towards Fred, and knock over all his carefully placed playthings while he cried out, 'She's 'turbing me!'

By this time Mother knew she would have to take Fred away from Broome, not from his sister – families have to cope with the advent of siblings – but from the climate, the sad vibrations from Dolly's death, the isolation and lack of health care. She was overwhelmed with the anxiety of possibly losing another child as Fred continued to weaken.

Grandpa, who had done so much for his daughter and son-in-law, insisted Mother go home for a holiday to regain her stamina. Dad had no choice but to let her go because of the position of financial reliance his marriage had put him in; he remained at home to keep up his business. We left for the long journey when I was one and Fred five, travelling by sea for a week to Perth, then four weeks to England. We went to the haven of my grandparents' home, New Farm, to tranquillity, beauty and an utterly different way of life. Granny employed a Norland nanny – the best – to look after me, giving Mother a rest from a demanding toddler and a chance to regain her health and heal her soul.

Observing the rapid improvement in Fred's fragile health in the soft English summer, Mother and her parents decided that he should remain at New Farm rather than return to Australia, and be sent to school by Granny and Grandpa, who doted on him and were still grieving the loss of their son, Billy. It was a terrible sacrifice for Mother to agree to leave Fred so far away for an unknown length of time, but for her it was the lesser of two evils. She felt she could not allow the Broome experience to go on any longer for him, so after a year in England she bravely returned to her life there with only her eternally robust daughter to accompany her.

As I grow older, memories of my childhood in Broome become clearer. The colours stand out strongly: the bare bright-red earth and brilliant red clustered heads of poinciana blossoms, hot pink and crimson oleanders and bougainvillea, the tangerine and gold of bird-of-paradise plumes. I remember harsh sunlight shimmering on the silver corrugated-iron sheds of Japtown and blasting white-hot off the sand on every beach except Riddell Beach, whose sand is orange-red.

Riddell is the next beach around from Cable; Gantheaume Point separates them. Pat Percy's lighthouse bungalow sat at the top of Gantheaume Point with an uninterrupted view of sparkling blue ocean. Below the house was a pool that Pat had carved out of scarlet rock-slabs for his ailing wife, Anastasia: the flowing tide bathed and soothed her aching rheumatic limbs. There was a time when Anastasia went to sea, pearl-fishing with her husband; in the howling cyclone of 1908 she was roped for safety to the mast of their lugger, *Gwendoline*; smaller boats were flung to the bottom of the ocean, fifty men were drowned, but the Pat Percys survived.

At Gantheaume Point dinosaur footprints have been left forever in the rock by a prehistoric creature 130 million years ago. I liked to imagine with a tingle of excitement these ancient creatures walking ponderously across the land.

Another great treat was to visit Ellies cafe and drink the famous lemon squash made on the premises from lemons, sugar and shaved ice. Drunk contentedly through straws from huge glasses, it was an inspired refreshment in the searing heat. Ellie himself was Ceylonese. He was very well liked and highly respected by the entire community, and became a world-renowned pearl cleaner.

Not so much fun were our visits to the Japanese market garden outside town to buy produce; the stench of the pigs in their sty near the entrance appalled me and I made a habit of pinching my nose and racing past them to where the fruit and vegetables grew beyond. Usually, however, a truck from the gardens would come by on call, about once a week, and Mother would buy anything we needed. The paw paws were my favourite.

In July and August the natural phenomenon of the Stairway to the Moon would thrill me. The huge yellow sphere of the full moon rises over Roebuck Bay just as the tide recedes, leaving shallow elongated strips of water behind on the seabed. The bright lunar light on the mudflats resembles a broad stairway leading right up to the moon, an invitation urging one to make the journey, I felt. In my dreams I climbed the stairs and melted into the moon-world, travelling through space as the gold turned to silver, then to mother-of-pearl white. At night an indigo sky glittered with innumerable stars, so close they shed a light of their own when there was no moon. Shooting stars fell constantly, some seeming to streak towards earth but suddenly darting back into the universe before landing.

One day, I saw something that challenged my cheery innocence: Aboriginal prisoners in khaki clothes, their ankles chained together. Sweat trickled down their faces; a confused expression showed in their sad eyes. I never saw this method of punishment again, it must have been stopped some time after that; but I never forgot it – it shocked me to the core.

I was an only child for several years, so quickly grew used to being the centre of attention until my sister Daisy was born in 1927. I later learnt that Mother nearly died after the birth, as she had haemorrhaged badly. I was not surprised when I was told that my father, desperate at the thought of losing her, had taken out a pistol and said to his friend, Broome's GP, 'There are two bullets in here. If you don't save her, you'll have one and I'll have the other.'

Mother also had at least one miscarriage during the five-year gap between Daisy and me, and I vaguely remember a time when Dad looked after me on his own. He pulled my white socks up crookedly, making me cross, and cleaned my teeth rather hard before we walked to the hospital to see Mother. White Broome men were not domesticated – looking after children was women's work in their eyes, and relegated to the maid if a nanny or the children's mother was not at hand. Perhaps at this time Jerry and Topsy were on walkabout.

I was jealous of Daisy, especially when Mother was breast-feeding her in the first few months after she was born. I would run away whenever I saw it, feeling alone and neglected, and would often do something naughty to attract her attention. Mother and I shared our own rituals though, one of which was stories at bedtime. I would lie on my bed in a corner of the mosquito room, watching as the glow from the candle lit up her face. In days long past before science had unravelled how a pearl-oyster creates a pearl, there were stories and legends from all over the world about their origin; I found them spellbinding. Some claimed they were found in the brains of frogs, or of dragons, and a fable translated from Sanskrit related how pearls formed from the tears of angels or water nymphs, combined with dewdrops, sunlight and the breath of air. This always reminded me of a favourite verse from Sir Walter Scott's *The Bridal of Triermain*:

> See these pearls, that long have slept;
> These were the tears by Naiads wept
> For the loss of the Marinel.
> Tritons in the silver shell
> Treasured them, till hard and white
> As the teeth of Amphitrite.

There were other pearl stories too, many of them found in a book I treasured, *The Book of the Pearl* (now long out of print). As I drifted off to sleep, dreaming of crystal-clear dew falling into shimmering pearl-shells floating on a smooth dawn ocean, Mother would sing to me in her soaringly beautiful voice. Our favourite hymn was one that contained the lines:

In this world of darkness so we must shine,
You in your small corner, and I in mine . . .

Among the jumble of my very early memories is the 1926 cyclone; I was four and a half. The day began ominously grey with increasing wind. I saw Dad carrying my friend Margot Field through the gate, her mother, Aunty Nell, behind them. Excitedly I asked Mother if Margot was coming to stay and she explained that a willy-willy was coming and that as Margot's father was away on business, Dad had brought them to be with us. We battened down for what seemed like a long time. The house was dark with all the shutters down, though dim lights shone from kerosene lanterns. Margot and I sat on potties – there was no question of going outside to the lavatory. There was the noise of devilish howling wind, of incessant rain drumming on the iron roof, but our house withstood the onslaught. Some didn't and were blown away, leaving the peculiar sight of cement steps going nowhere. We huddled together during this assault of nature, safe and dry. Dad was relieved: none of the luggers was lost because it was January, lay-up time.

My father's work was not something I thought about very much. I knew he had two offices, one in town and one at home. I sometimes watched him working in the home office to see what he was doing. It was a hot little room in which Dad would weigh the pearls collected from shell fished up during the fleet's latest expedition. He had a jeweller's magnifying glass, a monocle that he would scrunch into one eye and frequently wore attached to his shirt pocket by a black ribbon. He'd take out a pair of tweezers and tiny brass jeweller's scales, then concentrate on myriad pearls – many of which were seed pearls, which did not impress him. I was always amazed at the sweat that poured down his face while he worked. I often heard him mutter disgustedly, 'Barrack,' then thrust the offending baroque pearl to one side, as it was the perfectly round pearls that fetched real money. (I wonder now what those baroque pearls would be worth; fashion, ever fickle, has changed so that baroque beauties these days are highly prized, though they never match 'perfect' pearls for price.)

One day Dad took me with him to his office in town. On the way we stopped at the Roebuck Bay Hotel, where he must have arranged to meet some of his friends. Dad sat me on the bar while he ordered his beer from the pretty barmaid, and I watched with fascination the way the men chatted with her; they were charming, complimentary, flattering, and laughed and joked with her in a way I had never seen them behave with their wives. Dad must have rued the day he took me into that bar, as I later told Mother all about the nice things that had been said to the barmaid. I was never taken inside a Broome hotel again!

Dad sometimes told us stories about the divers and the expeditions on his luggers, and would explain to us how a diver prepared himself before descending to the ocean floor. I knew Grandpa Sprang manufactured the diving gear most of the divers used, so I listened with interest. The diver's tender and other attendants would help dress him, first in layers of clothing for warmth in the cold depths, then in the tough canvas diving dress, weighted boots and copper corselet. The copper diving helmet with the clean face-glass was finally screwed tightly into place. The tender, guardian of the diver's life, fitted the rubber air-pipe into the helmet, secured the lifeline around the diver's chest and signalled to the attendants to begin operating the pump-wheel, which hissed air into the helmet. Heavily descending the stout rope ladder from the lugger's deck, the shell-gatherer then threw himself into the sea, lifeline paying out slowly as he went down to the ocean floor.

There were many hazards facing the diver, Dad would tell us solemnly. One story I recall clearly is of a shark attack. One of Dad's divers was collecting pearl-oysters from a large outcrop that lay hidden among waving coral and clustering sponges. He was methodically placing each shell into a basket twelve fathoms under the sea in Broome waters. Suddenly he looked up and saw a huge tiger shark coming towards him through the murky water, its mouth agape and eyes cold and yellow. The copper diving helmet, thick canvas diving dress and heavy boots protected every part of the man inside except for his hands, which he concealed by clenching them in his armpits. The shark began to slowly circle its prey. The diver closed his air valve, allowing air pressure to expand the suit abnormally and release a stream of bubbles through the helmet's escape valve to scare the shark. Undeterred, the creature prepared to attack and rushed forwards as the diver's inflated suit began to lift him clear. Too late, frenzied razor-toothed jaws closed on the suit from behind, ripping out the seat. Air spurting through the torn cloth scared the shark momentarily, and before it could round on him again, the diver signalled frantically with his life-line to the boat above. Shooting to the surface like a cork, he was heaved onto the deck just as the shark streaked to the surface after him. Fortunately no serious injury was sustained by the diver as a result of this experience or from the sudden deflation of air pressure, which we knew could be deadly.

There were other hazards; air-pipes and lifelines could be fouled by sea creatures – whales trying to be friendly with luggers they mistook for another whale was a common story! Huge jellyfish trailing deadly stingers had to be avoided, and especially nasty were the devil rays, or giant 'sea bats', with enormous flapping wings and piggy eyes. Lethal sea snakes and the dreaded bends were just a couple more worries for the divers. Grandpa's gift to Broome of the decompression chamber in 1914 saved a significant number of lives from the bends. I learnt that if a diver's oxygen supply was cut, he stayed down too long, was unable to return to the surface by staging, or coming up in slow increments, the bends might claim him.

Dad's lugger Niobe
at his camp.

One of Dad's luggers
in Roebuck Bay.

Everyone in pearling, owners and crew alike, had to deal with unpredictable weather. A willy-willy or cyclone out of season, even simply a storm that was more turbulent than usual, could send a lugger and all souls on board to the bottom. It is sometimes scornfully said that master pearlers were 'verandah pearlers', sending others to sea while they sipped whiskeys and soda at home. How untrue; Dad would go out with his fleet for weeks at a time, dressed in fatigues, enduring the bad weather and cramped conditions like all his fellow master pearlers. He and the crew would work from sunrise to dusk every day, taking a rest day once a week, and at night, Dad and the diver would share a cabin, while the crew slept in hammocks. Ablutions were carried out on deck with a bucket of water. It was only when owners became too old to endure the rigours of life at sea that they directed proceedings from their offices or camps.

I was not allowed to accompany Dad on his luggers while he was working, but on special occasions we would go out on one for a picnic. I gained my sea legs at a very young age and was quite at home on the luggers. Pearling had stopped being a family show with wife and children on board by this time; it was considered big business and most certainly a man's world. Going out for a day-trip, though, was a popular pastime.

One day Mother, Dad and I drove to the foreshore camp on Dampier Creek and prepared to board Dad's boat, the *Niobe*, for a day's picnicking with family friends, the Lyons and the Secombes. Eighteen-month-old Daisy was left in the care of Topsy, as were the other toddlers for fear they'd fall overboard.

Niobe was resting in a watery trench waiting for the tide to come in. I climbed up the rope ladder onto the white beech deck, the others following behind me. Dad and the crew were already on board, packing the picnic baskets full of sandwiches, cake, beer and cordial into the covered deck shelter that led down to the two-bunk cabin where the master and Japanese diver slept when at sea.

The tide was swift, soon lifting *Niobe* until she was floating. Dad, arms waving, shouted orders to the crew, and I caught a glimpse of the anchor tattooed onto one of his freckled arms. The auxiliary motor going, we chugged into Dampier Creek through mangrove-lined water lanes. The water was alive with all sorts of creatures returning to the open sea on the neap tide: silvery bright fish, a ponderous turtle, velvety stingrays, sea snakes, dugongs, dolphins and tiger sharks. I knew there were crocodiles basking further down in Crab Creek among the tiny scurrying red crabs and big grey mud crabs that lived in the squelchy mangrove stubble, but we didn't see any that day. That was a relief, for their reptilian gaze chilled and repelled me. We cruised past the Chinese junk that two Frenchmen had sailed from Hong Kong on their way elsewhere; they'd dropped anchor in Broome for a few days.

Sails hoisted, we emerged from Dampier Creek into the blue of Roebuck Bay. To starboard was Streeters Jetty, surrounded by the leafy tops of the mangrove forests, home to colonies of bats, the trees nearly submerged by the tide. To port was Buccaneer Rock, bits of it still showing above the surface. We sailed up and around the jetty's end. I could see in the distance the barren and empty coastline, seemingly endless expanses of white sandy beach topped with low grey-green scrub. I loved looking at these familiar scenes from a different perspective.

The Filipino crewman at the tiller steered us out to sea, and we rocked to and fro on a gentle swell. Suddenly one heaving wave tipped *Niobe* sideways, but having been on luggers many times and knowing what to do, I held onto a mast until the lugger righted itself. The sun was fierce; I had on my cloth sou'wester to protect my freckled face from the glare and had to keep in the small shade provided by the lugger's canvas sails.

Mother and her friends unpacked the lunch but I was distracted by a pod of dolphins, which swam up to the lugger and frolicked beside us for a time. I had seen them a few times before and I loved their smiling faces. Transparent white jellyfish trailed long tentacles as they floated by and inquisitive fish streaked past; seagulls attracted by our lunch swooped down upon us and over and around the boat, demanding their share.

'Are you all right, Rosebuddy-budkin?' Dad inquired, a glass of beer in his hand.

'Yes, Daddy,' I assured him, my mouth full of egg sandwich.

I turned back to look out over the ocean. I was hoping to see some whales. Though I'd never seen one, Dad and his friends had many stories about encounters with them. They were powerful enough to tip a lugger up, and on one occasion, I was told, a curious whale had stood up on its tail next to the lugger so that it could look down and see what was going on on board. One of Dad's friends had also told me a story that touched me: he had woken in the cabin of his lugger one night to hear a whimpering that was like a baby crying, and the sound of something rubbing against the side of the boat. It had been a baby whale; probably it had lost its mother, and thought the lugger was her. I wondered what had happened to the poor baby whale.

I was contentedly drowsy after three hours of sea air and hot sun, as well as food and drink, so I was not unhappy when the man at the tiller turned *Niobe* for home; we had to return before the tide retreated from her mooring.

Our house was peaceful when my father was away at sea. For as far back as I can remember, my parents engaged in shouting matches, though neither was violent. I can't recall what the arguments were about, though I came to know that Dad was a difficult and jealous man, and the arguments disturbed me greatly. On one occasion, just after Dad had left to go to sea for an extended time, I was sleeping with Mother in her room inside the house. Suddenly the bedroom door crashed open and Dad appeared. Mother told me later that he had wanted to check whether there was anyone else in bed with her.

Whenever the shouting began, Tora and I would go out to

the back verandah and stand together. I always felt terribly protective towards my adored mother and at five or six years old, trembling but determined, I would walk inside and loudly tell Dad to stop being unkind. Taken aback by my boldness he'd reprimand me sternly, but he never spanked me. Later, during school holidays from boarding school, I paid for flouting him by being given three days CB (or 'Confined to Barracks', harking back to his army life), but somehow I'd always get out of it by the second day. As a young child I found the arguments very unsettling and was rather ambivalent towards my father. It took me years to realise that his difficult ways were the result of his unbearable wartime experiences, and the painful cutting of ties with his family and the way of life he had known in his childhood. Mother was not entirely blameless; all her friends told her she didn't know how to handle her husband, and I feel now that loving as she was, she had an actress's highly strung temperament which my father often found provocative.

When I turned five I began kindergarten. My first day and the days that followed are happy memories. The Roman

Catholic nuns from the St John of God convent ran the little school. There were no barriers among our widely differing religions in multicultural Broome; we were ecumenical before the word became fashionable. Later, whenever I was home for the holidays from my Church of England boarding school, my friends and I would be invited to the convent for afternoon tea with our beloved nuns who'd taught us in kindergarten. They were fascinated with our clothes, especially Pam's, as she always wore the latest fashions: 'Stand up, Pam darling, and let us see what they're wearing now!' Greeting and hugging their former pupils, our nuns would murmur sadly about some of us, 'Poor child!' I quietly asked Mother why we were 'poor', and she explained, 'Because you're not Roman Catholic. They believe you won't go to heaven.' She reassured me that I would!

We all loved Sister Alphonsus, who was young, pretty, very loving and full of laughter. On my first day of kindergarten I learnt to draw pot-hooks and can still feel the pencil between my fingers as I practised on lined paper. We sat in a row on little chairs: blond brothers Terry and Nolan McDaniel, Pam Gregory, Margot Field, Shirley Ogilvie and others about the same age. All the nuns wore head-to-ankle white habits, black wool stockings and black boots, even in the most sweltering months. Sometimes they would have a few days' stay at the remote Beagle Bay Mission further up the coast, where we discovered they'd go swimming. We asked, 'Do you wear those clothes in the water?' Sister Alphonsus chuckled and replied, 'No, we wear swimming costumes!' Oh! A nun in a swimming costume! Our minds boggled at the thought, but we were secretly pleased they were like everyone else under their habits.

Sometimes we tried to see if Sister Alphonsus had hair under her elaborate white veil. When sitting in a circle around her, a bold child, usually a boy, would furtively put out a finger and try to push up the front of Sister's veil, then we'd all join in, giggling, 'Have you hair, Sister?' It was a happy joke, and she would laugh with us.

I had my first proposal of marriage at kindergarten. Terry McDaniel said to me while we were sitting on our little chairs, 'Will you marry me, Buddy?' 'Yes, Terry,' I answered; he was a good-looking boy who grew to be a handsome man-about-town in Perth, but of course, the proposal was instantly forgotten by us both!

A big treat was to be chosen by Sister to go with her into the convent's chapel. Beckoning to me on lucky days, she'd hold my hand and we'd walk into a low white U-shaped building surrounding a green lawn, up wooden steps onto the verandah and through a door into another world, the colourful cool serenity of the chapel. There were beautiful life-size statues of Jesus and the Virgin Mary, flickering candles, relics and a lot of heavenly blue. Sister and I would kneel, she'd say a prayer and we'd light a candle, and she'd tell me about the chapel's contents, reverently taking out a little glass-fronted box from a sealed case. 'Here is a splinter from the true cross where Jesus was crucified,' she'd say.

Much later Sister Alphonsus became Mother Superior of the convent. I saw her beautifully tended grave in the white

Roman Catholic section of the Broome cemetery when I returned to my birthplace in 1996. She had died at a great age, having been loved by many generations of pupils, pre-schoolers and older children, including Asian and Aboriginal children, who were taught in a large open-sided canvas tent behind the convent, and who may not have had access to education without her little school.

Pam Gregory, Margot Field and I walked to kindergarten together. I left home first, stepping along the red-earth streets on my own, before stopping for Pam, then for Margot. There was no traffic and no fear of being molested in that innocent era: seething Japtown was never a threat and far away anyway. I was not allowed there on my own, however; Dad or Mother always drove me.

One morning Mother told me to pick up a friend's little boy on my way to kindergarten. He was younger than me, with a head of long golden corkscrew curls, his mother's pride. I was to walk with him until he could go by himself. The boy and I didn't pick up Pam or Margot but took a less roundabout route;

*Me (left) aged five, dressed as a violet,
and Pam, six, a fairy, at Margot Field's birthday party.*

we passed a small house with a straight path leading to the front gate, where one day I caught sight of something that made me pause. Bordering the path was a profusion of red, orange and yellow zinnias on tall stalks, which immediately enchanted me. I was overwhelmed by the wish to give some to my dear Sister Alphonsus so, telling my charge to wait, I opened the gate and walked up the path, picked some stems of the radiant blooms, and as I clutched them to me we continued on our way to school. I presented my bunch of flowers to Sister, who smiled, thanked me warmly and accepted them. When I arrived home from school Dad was waiting. He was very gentle and said, 'Rosebud, you picked someone's flowers today.' How did he know? I sensed something was wrong and replied simply, 'Yes, Daddy.'

'That's stealing, darling, and you mustn't do it again. You'll have to say you're sorry tomorrow and give the lady back her flowers.' I felt terribly ashamed and burst into tears, hating the idea of apologising for something I didn't know was wrong. Nevertheless, Dad drove me to the house the next morning while I held the bunch of zinnias – Sister must have rung, and my father had collected them. We knocked on the door and the lady opened it, smiling down at me. Red-faced, I handed her the flowers. I managed to say, 'I'm sorry I picked your flowers yesterday.' She bent down and kissed me, replying, 'Thank you for bringing them back.' Everyone was kind and understanding; to my relief the episode was never mentioned again.

My parents and their friends would meet at each other's houses for drinks at sundown most days and exchange news of the unstable price of pearl-shell. There was gossip, too. I must have taken into my subconscious the talk about my kindergarten charge's shoulder-length golden curls – the Broome men disapproved, expecting boys to be boys. One day after school when the little boy came home with me to play, I said, 'Let's play barbers.' He happily agreed, so we went into the bathroom; he sat on a chair, I found a pair of scissors and tucked a large towel around his neck. Taking the scissors I carefully and professionally, I thought, cut off his beautiful ringlets. When my young friend went home his mother was devastated. I wasn't scolded – Dad was proud of me; he told the story for years, and all his friends laughed and applauded my action. I don't know why I was so bold, and I'm not at all proud of what I did.

We spent most of these sundown hours, and many others as well, with the Gregorys. Aunty Kate and Greg, Pam's parents, were Mother and Dad's closest friends. Two young couples with everything in common, they'd counsel one another through blazing rows as well as enjoy the good times together. One night when Mother and Dad were dining with the Gregorys, Pam and I were put down on the big double bed under a speeding ceiling fan and promptly fell asleep. Much later, when it was time to call it a night, the four friends trooped along the verandah into the bedroom and picked us up. Not half a minute later the heavy wooden fan, its blades still whizzing lethally, suddenly fell onto the bed exactly where we'd been lying. It would have killed us instantly if we'd still been there. Mother often talked about this strange incident. Our guardian angels must have been watching over us, she said.

On another occasion, the Gregorys and Goldies were relaxing at the Pat Percy 'Lighthouse', the only house at Gantheaume Point above Riddell Beach. It was rented out for holidays and day use, and had an uninterrupted view over the Indian Ocean. Pam was about five and I was four. The grownups were having lunch when one of us ran onto the verandah, excitedly calling, 'Come and see the pretty worm!' Our parents left the table and rushed outside. One of us was gently patting a multicoloured snake, which lay rigid and was probably terrified. Greg and Dad snatched us away and dispatched the reptile immediately. Pam and I were left with a phobia of snakes, but we don't know, even now, which of us patted the creature – probably we both did.

Around this time, I was taken to Broome hospital to have my tonsils out. I'd suffered from bouts of 'stiff neck', for which I was put in a cane easychair with green oilcloth wrapped around my neck. One day I was sitting on Mother's knee having a cuddle when Dad came in. Mother hugged and kissed me and I was carted off to our car, in which several men were sitting.

Unaware, though suspicious of the unusual proceedings, I sat between two strangers on the back seat – the surgeon and surgeon's assistant, as it turned out. Dad drove and we all got out at the little hospital. The next thing I knew I was being forced to lie down on a white-covered table with a huge round white light blazing down on me. I got up to flee this chamber of horrors, but my flailing legs were held down tightly while an evil-smelling mask was clamped over my face and the horrible sensation of losing consciousness under ether enveloped me. Blue circles flashed, growing bigger and bigger, ringing noises sounded; then I knew no more until I woke up with a dreadfully sore throat. I was on a bed on my own in a latticed room.

What I didn't know until I was older was Dad's story of the operation: he was sitting outside the theatre when he noticed there was a lot of panicky rushing about. It was common knowledge that his beloved friend, the local doctor, had a drinking problem and tended to grow steadily more inebriated as the day wore on. He'd been a brilliant student, topping his final year at Sydney University, but had taken to the bottle after his wife's death; in many ways he was a typical Broome desperado, a lost soul both accepted in and beguiled by the frontier town. My father certainly thought him the best doctor in the world. Unfortunately, he overdid the ether during my operation and my heart stopped, but the team of doctors managed to revive me (and he and my father remained great friends).

The surgeon, who travelled along the coast once a year to perform operations, 'guillotined' my tonsils in his haste to get the job completed before disaster could strike again, and made a mess of my throat. Subsequent doctors, especially the English ones who pulled my tonsils out properly some years later, tut-tutted over the state of the area ever after.

Before World War I countless coloured lanterns had lit Japtown at night. Some were tiered and tasselled in multiple colours, others, round and red; it was said to be a beautiful sight. Broome has not relied on lantern-light when darkness falls since electricity came to town when I was a small child. I watched technicians installing the magic switch that turned on the instant light in our house. However, there was still one night of the year when handmade Japanese creations were alight again. *Tsuki Miro*, the Festival of the Lanterns, was held during the first full moon in August, the biggest moon of the year. Local Japanese gave pearling families two or three of their wonderful lanterns and we hung ours in the verandah sitting room to admire. They were delicate, fanciful works of art, the paper crimped, pleated and decorated with diamond-bright miniature mirrors and tiny ornaments. Thick silk tassels and strings of shimmering glass beads dangled gracefully from them.

Celebrations of remembrance were held in the cemetery during the festival, and when I was six, my parents took me to see them. The ceremony greeted the spirits of dead divers whose souls returned to earth at moonrise and mingled with their mourning relatives and friends until midnight. The pearling fleets returned to Broome for this annual event. I watched wide-eyed as Japanese men in armour fenced with long poles, their movements dictated by ancient rules, the scene lit by glowing lanterns in the trees. On the graves lay offerings of small round pink and green cakes, bottles of liquor and burning joss-sticks. The spicy scent wafted far, and still teases my nostrils now. Japanese women wearing flowered silk kimonos, white socks dividing the big toe from the others and *zori* thongs on their feet, fluttered their fans while swaying in ritualistic movements, communing with the shades of the departed.

After the ceremony we drove to the foreshore, where 'soul boats', tiny replicas of luggers crafted for the Japanese who had died that year, were launched into the waters of Roebuck Bay. They were beautiful models, about eighteen inches long, with sails and exquisite tiny lantern lights. They were filled with scented flowers and favourite morsels of food. Each boat was carefully placed on the outgoing tide to the ringing of bells and chanted prayers, and everyone watched until they disappeared. It was said that if a boat sailed straight out to the horizon the departed soul was happy, but if it was wrecked or veered off to one side, things were not right with the soul. That year, one of the boats had been made for Fat Charlie, who had kept a brothel and been a go-between for stolen pearls on the snide market – a generally shady character and part-time diver who had just died. His soul boat sailed right out to the horizon, but all the others veered left – it was the talk of the town.

My mother, like the other Europeans in Broome, gave dinner parties during the festival, and Tora would stuff a large freshly caught kingfish with breadcrumbs, lemon juice, onions and lemongrass, salt and pepper. It was cooked in the kerosene oven in a large baking dish, basted with tinned butter, for about twenty minutes, then some of Dad's tomatoes were sliced and spread over the top and it would go back in for another forty minutes. It was served with sprouts from the Japanese market garden and Tora's fluffy boiled rice, and was utterly delicious. Mother always said Tora's rice was the best she'd ever tasted; I'm not sure what his secret was, but he let it boil over in messy streaks down the saucepan sides, which he'd have to scour clean every time.

One year something different happened at the cemetery. While the ceremony was taking place, groups of Aborigines watching unseen in dense surrounding bush saw an opportunity to play a joke on the 'Japs' and get some of their own back, for it was widely known that the Japanese habitually mistreated the Aboriginal men and women. When everyone had left and the cemetery was dark and quiet, shadowy figures moved among the tombstones, tasting the food, quaffing the alcohol and generally having a high time. When the prank was discovered, the Japanese were furious. The next year, bottles of spirits were cemented alongside the graves up to their necks. Once more, Aborigines hid silently among the trees until all was dark and quiet, then they moved in, knelt with grass straws in their mouths and drained the bottles dry, laughing among themselves at so easily fooling 'the arrogant Jap man'. When the story spread around Broome, everyone chuckled at their resourcefulness.

The mixture of races in Broome sometimes caused problems, though 'live and let live' was the attitude of most people when I was growing up there. The Aboriginal camp next door to our house was an enclave of its own, and Japtown was also over-whelmingly non-white. There were riots caused by racial tensions between the Japanese and the Dutch East Indian Koepangers (Timorese) in 1920–21, though nothing like it ever happened again. Four Koepangers and two Japanese were killed. There were always stories of vendettas between individuals, espe-cially over pearls, and a few murders, all confined to Japtown. Aborigines had their fights too, especially on corroboree nights.

One night I was padding unobtrusively in bare feet around a group of my parents' friends, who were having after-dinner drinks in the verandah sitting room. The sounds of harsh singing and clapsticks wafted in louder and louder on the hot night air from next door. Suddenly Tora shot out of the kitchen, agitated and screeching, 'Missus, come quick, big black man at door, all bloody, bin fight.' Mother got up and fol-lowed Tora, and I did too, curious to see what was going on. At the bottom of the back-door steps stood a very tall Aborig-inal man, his face covered by a hessian curtain on a string. He lifted it to reveal his coal-black face, which was streaming bright with blood from a mass of cuts. 'Missus, I bin fight over lubra, man cut me.' He came into the kitchen and sat down.

Mother must have done what she could for him, but I did not wait around to find out.

One day Pam Gregory showed me a photo of her parents taken when they'd first returned to Broome after their marriage in Perth. They were sitting on either side of a cane table on their lattice-enclosed verandah. I was struck by their beauty, they were both tall, elegant, she stunningly pretty, he was very handsome. Kate was wearing a long skirt and frilly blouse, her hair caught up at the nape of her neck; Greg wore a master pearler's land outfit, a white linen jacket with pearl-shell buttons, gold studs at the throat and white trousers. They were a head-turning couple.

Both of them adored Pam, and she them. Sadly, the marriage didn't last and Kate left Broome; like many Broome wives, she was chafing against the small-town isolation, and had grown tired of Greg's flirtatious ways. Pam was enrolled at Perth College, spending holidays with her mother and grandparents in their big house on the Swan River, and during the long Christmas holidays she would stay with her father in Broome.

*The photo Pam showed me: Captain Ancell and Kate Gregory
are served afternoon tea by their houseboy in Broome.*

At first tearful, then angry, Pam eventually characteristically
decided to turn the upheaval into an adventure. I was six when
Pam left Broome; she was seven. We were not to see each other
again for another five years.

I missed Pam when she left, but I still had other good
friends: twins Sheila and Flora Milner, Laurel Everett, Shirley
Ogilvie and Margot Field. Margot's parents, Aunty Nell and
Uncle Charles, were also close friends of my parents. Margot
inherited her mother's colouring – both were dark-haired
beauties – and her father's wit, and we were happy playmates,
about the same age. One of our pastimes was to dress up in
Nell's old frocks from a big box at Margot's house, then we'd

fill a bath with cold bore water, get in and eat peeled mangoes while our dresses floated up to our collarbones. Perhaps it was a way of cooling off in the heat and staying clean while sucking the dribbly fruit from their big stones.

Another memorable treat was a luscious ice-cream made for one of my birthday parties from rich, thick, vanilla custard; of course there was none to be bought in the town. It was hand-churned in a large steel container packed with ice and embraced by barefoot Jerry, reclining on the red soil, his back against a gum tree, the churn held firmly horizontal between his outstretched legs. He slowly turned the handle with one hand for a long time in the hot early afternoon. The resulting creamy ice confection was smooth and fragrant.

My friends and I saw each other every day at kindergarten, but also often went to Town Beach in the evening, with or without our parents; as night fell we'd splash in the shark-netted pool, watching our bodies sparkle with veils of cobwebby phosphorous. There was no thought of danger from anyone; our isolated backwater was everybody's playground, vast, empty, ours. One day, as we approached Town Beach, our little crowd of boys and girls, aged six to ten, saw rows of huge turtles lined up on the shore, half burrowed into the sand. Somebody uncovered a clutch of eggs from under an unprotesting turtle. They were soft and malleable, no hard shells, so more were dug from the sand. Egg fights followed – we all joined in, ignorant and unthinking. Then we tried eating them, although raw, and thought how nice they were, just like hen's eggs but better and slightly different. I even took some home. At last we left and I don't know if turtles have ever returned to lay their eggs at Town Beach.

The most beautiful trees I have ever seen are the poincianas that grow in Broome. They're tall, smothered in a blaze of fiery blooms during the summer, their delicate frondy green foliage only seen in tufts here and there; they must have a special affinity with the bright red Broome earth that nourishes them. Although native to Peru, and introduced to other hot climates, the ones I've seen elsewhere have never matched the poincianas of my birthplace in height, width or abundance of flowers.

I spent a lot of time at Sheila and Flora Milner's house, further up from us on Walcott Street. The house was shaded by a spreading tamarind tree, and there was also a beautiful poinciana tree. My friends had a wooden cubby-house nailed to its sturdy branches. We would climb up the tree and sit on the planks of the cubby, surrounded by a haze of saucer-size ruby blossoms, the clear sky above seen in blue patches through occasional gaps in the flowery canopy. We chattered, laughed and played happily for hours, plucking and eating the one creamy-gold petal from among the four red ones in each cluster – Flora told us this petal was edible.

Sheila and Flora were not identical twins. Sheila looked like her tall Irish mother, Catherine, a cool blonde with twinkly blue eyes and a sense of fun. Flora took after her father, marine engineer Harry, a long-legged and good-looking Irishman; she had light brown curly hair framing a gamin face and dancing hazel eyes. She was a free spirit, irrepressible, impish, bubbling with ready laughter. Both, like me, were covered with freckles.

Flora was wise about the bush. We'd roam together through thickets of scrubby grey native plants, Flora telling us which leaves and berries to nibble; she rescued lost wild creatures and nurtured them until they could fend for themselves. At one time a sulphur-crested cockatoo accompanied us everywhere, but unusually it loved Sheila and hated Flora – she said the feeling was mutual. Sheila's tabby cat kept its claws sheathed with difficulty and avoided the bird. Another of Flora's orphans was a joey, which lived inside the front of her shirt just as it would have lived in its mother's pouch. Now and again it would jump out, hop about the grass for a bit, then leap back inside Flora's top. She gave it milk from a tiny bottle with a teat. She took it everywhere, even to Sunday School in the tiny Anglican Church of the Annunciation where, when he was in town, lovely Bishop Frewer, whom we affectionately called Bish, would tell us stories from the Bible.

The rest of the weekend was spent at each other's houses, or playing with our gang of friends at Town Beach. Sometimes, our family would venture further afield by car, to visit friends on one of the huge Kimberley land-holdings that extended almost to the fringes of our little urban island.

Surrealist painters like Salvador Dali would have revelled in the unbelievable colours, weird rock shapes and striking trees on the way to Roebuck Plains Station, managed by Kim and Joy Male, old friends of my parents. We would travel about twenty miles out of Broome on bone-shaking rough tracks through stark country where cattle grazed on sparse tufts of grass. Settlements of monolithic scarlet anthills rose on all sides from the pindan and we'd drive on, mile after mile, until we reached the homestead. It would suddenly appear in the distance, clumps of trees with dense foliage protecting and hiding the rambling, iron-roofed house.

Driving through the garden gates an oasis was revealed: smooth emerald-green lawns surrounded by tall trees, leafy shrubs, bright flowers, blazing bougainvillea. Joy had been an elegant Perth girl from a well-known family, the Lathlanes, before her marriage. She was a pioneering woman of great character, smartly dressed, the life of the party. There were no quick plane trips to Perth – or anywhere else – in those days and one had to be self-reliant and resourceful. Joy was both, and had transformed a barren plot into a lush haven in the middle of nowhere.

The house had wide verandahs and airy rooms, and I recall that 'walls' of dampened hessian were hung when the heat was unbearable. On one visit, I was trying to sleep in one of these hessian-lined rooms but had a terrible head cold. I decided to dry out my sopping wet handkerchief over a candle flame, but it promptly caught alight. I must have screamed, for the adults quickly put out the fire, though I hate to think what would have happened if the flames had reached the hessian.

When my father's pearling lugger *Rosef* cast off from Broome's jetty on the night of 1 April 1929, she was not on her way to the pearling grounds, but sailing on a very different mission. Tradewinds filled the vessel's mainsail, the auxiliary engine pumped, and the usual Asian crew worked hard to hurry *Rosef* towards a waiting coastal steamer. SS *Minderoo*, anchored further out in deep water, was a thrilling fairyland of sparkling lights floating on the dark ocean. She was headed south, to Perth. I have a vivid memory of that night, and can still see the pools of golden light on the timber decking at my feet; the radiance came from a kerosene lantern lashed to the riding mast. Suddenly the boat tilted sideways at a crazy angle as she rode a heavy swell. I instinctively pressed my back hard against a stationary piece of deck equipment to stop sliding down the deck into the foaming scuppers.

In a surge of excitement I looked up at the stars, thinking, I'm seven years old tonight and I'm going to England! Dad, Mother and two-year-old Daisy were on *Rosef* too. Dad was coming with us to Perth while we waited at the Esplanade Hotel for SS *Ceramic* to dock at Fremantle and take Mother, Daisy and me on the long trip to England. The visit had been much longed for by my grandparents, as Mother was exhausted and nervy, the arguments with Dad worsening, and Daisy, who they'd never seen, was a frail baby. Dad was not coming; after seeing us off, he would return to Broome and his pearling boats on the next ship going north.

Minderoo had been held up at Derby and was committed to schedules along the coast. She had been unable to tie up at Broome's long wooden jetty; the receding thirty-foot tide had left the tall wharf standing high above exposed grey mud, and the ocean was only now beginning to race back in, allowing our lugger to float. As often happened, it was more expedient for a lugger to pick up travellers, cargo and mail from the jetty's lower landing while there was enough water to keep her afloat, and then rendezvous with the ship well away from land. Sometimes the liner or steamer would send her own lifeboat to do the job if a lugger was not available, and if time and tide fitted into the schedule it would come alongside the jetty for an extended stay, sitting high and dry when the ocean departed, in a shallow trench of seawater on the sludgy mud. Once, Dad and I walked out to a boat from the shore in our sandshoes, passing sea-life stranded in puddles – starfish, jellyfish, sea-slugs, tiny crabs and small panicking fish – squelching our way around the upright ship that looked out of place, like a beached monster from the deep. Wasting no time, we hurried back towards dry land before a stray crocodile or the incoming tide overtook us.

Rosef kept up her pace, rolling on the waves while puffs of wind carried lingering scents of oleander and frangipani, the flowers' sweet fragrance contrasting with whiffs of mangrove mud. But as we sped onwards, blustery sea air blew away the last reminders of the shore. *Minderoo*'s brightly lit outline became clearer and clearer until at last we drew alongside the towering ship, the wooden lugger bumping and scraping against the steamer's steel plates. A canvas-lined gangway was already in place, stout ropes were thrown by our crew to waiting sailors, who secured our tiny bobbing craft, the men shouting good-humoured instructions and interesting swear words to one another. Firm hands helped us leap over the inky sea between lugger and ship (a safety net slung below) and onto the gangway's solid duckboard where balance was regained. We walked up to steady sheltered decks and were shown to our snug cabin, where the rivet-studded walls were painted gleaming white and clean linen sheets were folded flat on hard bunks. I noticed a strong clean smell, peculiar to spotless ships' cabins.

Our parents put us to bed, turned out the light and shut the door, wanting to walk around the decks. I would have liked to go too but was tired and ready to settle down. I remember the sensation of my body between the smooth, cool sheets and, eyes closed, I heard the rattle of anchor chains and the steady heartbeat of the engines, felt the gentle rocking of the ship, and slept soundly till morning.

There were many children of different ages on board the *Minderoo*. For the toddlers there was a nursery, which contained toys and a rocking horse and was presided over by a stewardess in a white uniform. The older children ran boisterously all over the ship, egging each other on; we climbed noisily up and down companionways between decks, looked down air vents trying to see people in their cabins below, played card games and deck quoits. The weather remained fine, but at times the seas were rough and huge and foam-flecked waves rocked our small vessel.

I knew I had travelled to England before, but could not remember anything about that time. It was five years since Mother had last seen Fred; I did not remember him at all. He had never seen Daisy, who could scarcely believe in the existence of her big brother. And of course Dad had not seen his only son for more than six years, and it would be longer still before he saw him again.

On this journey, a week after we left Broome, *Minderoo* arrived at Fremantle wharf. Disembarking, we were driven to the comfortable Esplanade Hotel, a favourite base in Perth for country people. It overlooked the Swan River, which was alive with all kinds of craft. I liked walking on the hotel's plush red carpet and riding in the birdcage lift. Life was a civilised and pleasant experience during that brief period. A temporary nanny came to look after Daisy and me; she took us for walks to green parks and to the Botanic Gardens, where we fed swans on a lake, and best of all, for ferry rides across the river to South Perth and the zoo.

Late one evening we boarded the *Ceramic* and settled into our 'bibby' cabin, a compartment with a narrow passage down one side and a porthole at the end. A steward came and explained the let-down washbasins and other features, and then we had to say goodbye to Dad, which I hardly remember in all the excitement. The ship set a course westwards and steamed away into the Indian Ocean and a different life began.

Being on board the *Ceramic* was like living in a self-contained town at sea; the purser's office, known as the 'barber's shop' was stocked with just about anything one would need for the eight-week journey. After what seemed like a long time, *Ceramic* berthed at Durban in South Africa.

Mother, Daisy and I moved into the Balmoral Hotel, a beautiful resort on one of Durban's beaches, for three days while *Ceramic* took on a load of coal. We breakfasted on a terrace, looking through archways to the sand and sea where we played and bathed. We went for tram rides and saw a pet monkey on a verandah. In the streets the Zulus, huge black men impressive in colourful feather headdresses and ankle decorations, pulled rickshaws, gracefully running and jumping high into the air and floating slowly down to earth again as they loped along. I was carried away by the sight and kept begging Mother to take us for a ride, but she'd always reply firmly, 'White women have been known to disappear forever in one of those rickshaws.'

When we arrived back at the docks to board *Ceramic* again, a strange scene was unfolding. Laughing black boys were diving for pennies from the wharf as passengers flung the coins into the sea as the ship pulled away. The youths would triumphantly hold up a penny every time they retrieved one, then put the coins in their mouths for safekeeping.

The *Ceramic* steamed on her way, around the Cape of Good Hope, and on into the South Atlantic Ocean heading for Cape Town. One night the ship stopped the engines and dropped anchor. In the dark we were suddenly surrounded by small craft and heard loud, chattering voices. Local merchants were waiting to climb on board and display their wares before passengers could get to the shops in port. Sure enough, by the time we were up the next morning, all kinds of exciting goods were spread on colourful mats over the main deck. The merchants still on board, *Ceramic* pulled into Cape Town.

There was great excitement on deck. In the sunshine Table Mountain rose high and square above the town, so close I could see and hear, to my amazement, dozens of creamy-brown mountain goats running nimbly along its slopes, hooting loudly. Just then a filmy white cloud enveloped the lofty summit and Mother exclaimed, 'Look at the tablecloth on Table Mountain!' This phenomenon was well known, she said.

We went ashore for the day, rode in an open green touring charabanc and later got into a black horse-drawn hansom cab, the driver pulling back a shutter in the roof to speak to us. The vehicle clattered over cobblestones to the quay. It was all different and exciting to me.

The ship stayed in port overnight, and when the engines began to hum early the next morning I ran from my bunk to the porthole at the end of our cabin to watch *Ceramic* leave

Cape Town. The sea was dark, but as the sun rose the choppy waves turned a magical raspberry-red. It lasted only a moment, then the ocean returned to its usual blue.

Tenerife, one of the Canary Islands, was the next port, and we went ashore on a launch. I recall the sunlight shining on pastel-coloured buildings of pink, lemon and blue, and laughed to see donkeys wearing straw hats, their long ears comically poking through specially cut openings. We went to the markets, which smelt of exotic overripe fruit, and a car took us to the top of a mountain where a freezing misty rain fell.

On board once more, we were finally steaming towards England. One day Mother pointed excitedly to some land and said, 'Look! The Isle of Wight!' Then a thick fog closed in and the ship stopped altogether, foghorns sounding incessantly all around us. At last, we pulled into Southampton. On deck Mother held Daisy, weeping and calling out, 'Mummy! Daddy!' as she waved to two elderly people standing close together on the wharf. I hadn't known until then that people could cry for joy.

We went by train to Bromley Station and were taken by car to New Farm, the most beautiful place I had ever seen and one that changed my life forever.

Part III

England, 1929–33

When we swept through the big open gates of New Farm and motored down the long gravel driveway to the pillared entrance of my grandparents' old Georgian house, it was as though my spirit had come home. I walked inside as naturally as if I'd never left. In the wide hall Patch, the family fox terrier, jumped as high as me, thrilled to bits to have more children around, and the cat, Tinker, with his shiny black coat, purred and rubbed himself against my legs, his knowing golden eyes showing he remembered past times.

Daisy and I had both caught whooping cough on the *Ceramic*. Frail Daisy's had been serious, with her weak chest and nightly croup, but we received the best care and both recovered. I recall caught breath and uncontrollable loud whoops. When we'd settled down on the day of our arrival, after lunch and a rest, Granny felt we should make the most of the long summer afternoon and get some fresh air and sunlight, so we had tea on the far lawn where trees were not casting shadows over us. She said: 'Queenie will bring out a tray.' I'd never heard that name before and was impressed. Smiling Queenie eventually appeared with the tea things. She wore a black dress, thick black stockings, black lace-up shoes, a white lacy band threaded with black ribbon across her forehead and a short frilly white apron to match – I thought it a very strange outfit. We sat on a thick rug and ate delicious buttered scones and slices of Dundee cake; the grown-ups drank tea and Daisy and I had glasses of barley water. In the soothing surroundings I listened to buzzing industrious bees and bell-like tinkles from small birds; smelt soft sweet scents; basked in gentle sunshine under a powder-blue sky flecked here and there with tiny woolly clouds. I noticed with interest the light and dark green stripes on the grass left by the motor mower and smoothed by a huge roller pushed by Bowler, the second gardener. Granny and Mother talked quietly about grown-up things while Daisy played on the rug and I soaked up the peace.

From the start it seemed to me that England had a fragrant scent, something subtle, unique, unforgettable, which would inspire in me a deep nostalgia for the rest of my life. Everything struck me as being in complete contrast to Broome: the soft light, the restful harmonious atmosphere, the musical chirping of countless birds, the mossy-green lawns, velvety to lie on. Life was ordered, predictable and privileged in every way. We children were fortunate with our surroundings – nowhere within the garden was out of bounds – and there was so much to see and take in. In Broome, there had been no real boundaries, but always a sense of isolation, remoteness and limitless horizons, which can make you a little uneasy.

I began exploring my new home immediately. Once a working farm with substantial acreage, New Farm had been broken up into large estates with big houses on them when I lived there. The original graceful, ivy-covered house was surrounded by four and a half acres of garden, not a large one by English standards of the time, but highly regarded for its fine horticultural beauty and quality. Grandpa, a member of the Royal Horticultural Society, took enormous pride in the garden and opened the New Farm grounds once a year for charity.

Entering the house via a classic outdoor porch, you'd find

yourself in a spacious hall with rooms opening off it and a broad curving staircase at the end. To the left of the staircase was a door to the elegant formal drawing room. As it was summer, the long French doors were hung with a light material; in winter dark green velvet curtains took their place. Armchairs were covered in chintz, which was removed in colder weather. The French doors opened on two sides of the room to a paved terrace roofed in sloping glass, and trained underneath were wisteria vines, knotted bare branches in winter, a dense mauve haze of hanging blooms in spring, shady green leaves in summer, then a golden leafy canopy in autumn. There was also a morning room, a dining room and at the back of the house an enormous kitchen complete with scullery, larders, cool rooms, and a cooking range running the length of one wall, all presided over by cheerful Mrs Bowler.

Our bedrooms were upstairs. Granny and Grandpa had a big carpeted bedroom that stretched nearly the entire length of the house. Their bathroom was next door in those days before ensuites, and Grandpa had a dressing room as well. Daisy and I shared a long room decorated in rose pink and grey, and our cousin Kitty would sleep there too when she was at New Farm. There were four beds, each with a rose brocade bedspread and grey taffeta eiderdown. Fred had a room to himself across the hallway, and there was a guest room next to ours in which I would later do my homework and practise ballet when we didn't have visitors staying. Along the hall was a large bathroom that we children shared with Mother and visitors.

The house was not at all like the one I'd lived in in Broome;

New Farm's Georgian house.

to my seven-year-old mind it was so much nicer, so much more civilised – but it was New Farm's garden that really inspired me. It was divided into 'rooms' with immaculate lawns and summer-houses thoughtfully placed for rest, shelter and observation. There was a large brick-walled kitchen garden with an enchant-ing arched gateway, through which there was another rolling lawn where summer tennis could be played, the nets stowed away between seasons. There was a 'wild' garden, where I came across my first moss roses with their tightly crinkled pink petals and 'moss'-covered buds. Grandpa's renowned herbaceous bor-ders, descending in tiers above pathways to a sunken garden with a sundial, were colourful and fragrant. Old-fashioned flowers and cottage-garden simples grew there – carnations, pinks, hypericum, violets, perennial chamomile daisies, and others I didn't know the names of. There were also glasshouses for seedlings and rare plants. Well away from the house, and separated from it by a long high hedge, were a huge old barn from farming days (we children played there in wet weather) and great pieces of agricultural equipment that were no longer used. As you walked out of the barn on the other side there was a series of low buildings. The Bowlers lived in one and in another apples were stowed after harvesting and garden utensils were kept.

There were two entrances to New Farm: imposing double gates at the front opened onto Westmoreland Road, the back gates onto Hayes Road, with Bromley Common rising behind it. As you entered the front gate there was a field with an old horse in it on one side of the driveway and an orchard on the other, filled with ancient gnarled fruit trees growing among long grasses and wildflowers. The high fence along Westmoreland Road sheltered enormous old horse chestnuts massed with pink and white 'candle' flowers in summer, followed in autumn by conkers, the spiky green outer shells that cover the shiny brown chestnuts. The shells would split open and let the conkers fall to the ground, ready for children to throw at one another. Later, my friends and I would often play after school among the low branches of the horse chestnuts, laughing and shouting and plunging in and out among these beautiful, stately trees. One day Grandpa, taking his usual afternoon walk around his beloved garden and hearing the laughter, came to where we were playing and said to me with a twinkly smile lighting up his usually rather melancholy face, 'Rosemary, it makes me happy to hear you and your friends enjoying yourselves among the trees, that is what this garden is for!' I was relieved – I'd thought we were going to be told off for being too noisy!

The long driveway ended in a wide circle with a lawn in the middle, in which grew a tall holly tree with glossy green leaves, brilliant red berries clustering among them in winter. Sitting in the dining room for lunch or afternoon tea, we would sometimes see a busy woodpecker working away at the bark.

My grandfather loved to encourage birds to the garden – there were bird tables for lean times and coconuts hung in the trees, a hole cut into them so birds could shelter in the winter months and peck at the flesh when food was scarce. There was a special garden seat with a favourite verse carved into the wood along the back: 'The kiss of the sun for pardon, the song of the birds for mirth, you are closer to God in a garden, than anywhere else on earth.'

I cannot recall all the trees and shrubs that grew at New Farm, but I do remember cherished laburnums, 'golden rain', whose blooms hung down like wisteria, and lilac trees, especially one gloriously abundant and sweetly scented white one. Old oak trees abounded and there was one enormous one, much venerated, which was said to be five hundred years old. There were ancient yew trees whose bark was black and sooty with age. We were told not to touch them, otherwise our clothes would be horribly stained, which they were a few times.

There were roses everywhere. I used to gaze into them deeply to try to see baby fairies, and there was great excitement when one day I was convinced I'd seen one curled up in the heart of a pale pink, newly opened rose. Others grew in the kitchen garden, which was a magic place that captured within its walls the atmosphere of past centuries. At the entrance was a high thick rose bush covered with small white double blooms. The sweet fragrance overwhelmed me and I stood by the bush for a long time, enthralled. Inside this enchanted world climbing cabbage roses twined their way along hanging chains across the paths, their huge pink blooms also sweetly scented. I was told that they were over one hundred years old. Espaliered peach trees that bore sun-ripened fruit were trained against a wall, Grandpa's pride and joy. Brick footpaths led to bushes of berries – gooseberries, redcurrants, blackcurrants, white currants, rows of scarlet strawberries, canes of crimson raspberries – beds of asparagus, potatoes, peas, beans, brussels sprouts, spinach and culinary herbs. Sunny beds held bushes of powerfully scented thyme, their flowers in spring and summer attracting honey bees and clumsy bumblebees. Marjoram and sage tumbled amongst the thyme. Parsley, spearmint and tall angelica grew in shadier parts.

I'm still amazed at the huge impact this earthly paradise had on every atom of my being. I longed for it ever afterwards, and indeed, many years later at our home in Dural, Somerset Cottage, the essence of New Farm's gardens existed again.

A few days after our arrival at New Farm, we were reunited with Fred. I had always known that Daisy and I had a brother; Mother talked about him and I was curious to know what he was like. Mother had written long letters to him – one of her friends remembered that she even wrote during bridge games when she was dummy. When Fred arrived home to New Farm from his prep school for the summer holidays, I saw a freckled little boy with light brown hair, blue eyes and knobbly knees below short trousers. He saw a wispy little girl freckled all over, reddish hair pulled back with a large bow, and dressed in a flowered Liberty frock. Neither of us felt any emotion; we just stared, sizing each other up. Fred barely remembered me. He had been six when Mother and I had returned to Broome from England; I'd been two and had no memory at all of him. Now at ages seven and eleven it seemed we had nothing in common.

Our cousin Kitty arrived shortly afterwards. Kitty, an only child, was also at boarding school but her mother, my Aunt Gay, wanted her to be included in New Farm life, so she usually came to Granny and Grandpa to spend most of the holidays with Fred. Since living at New Farm, Kitty had grown up with Fred. With only two years age difference, they were like brother and sister, but because I had no memory of Fred and no attachment to him, I wasn't at all envious of their relationship. I had no recollection of Kitty either, and we had to make friends with each other. She was a pretty girl with long dark ringlets to her shoulders, deep blue eyes, matt white skin and pink cheeks. She was nearly two years older than me, taller, self-contained, sometimes aloof. I admired her at once.

Fred and Kitty in the garden at New Farm in the late 1920s.
Bowler mows the lawn in the background.

Kitty and Fred's holiday playmate was Fred's best friend, Roy Marchand, who lived next door. His parents were Swiss and the family were living in England for business reasons. Roy was tall and good-looking, and I thought he was rather special, though to my chagrin he seemed to prefer Kitty. On one particularly painful occasion, Fred told Roy, 'Buddy's in love with you!' Mortified, I blushed beetroot red and ran upstairs to my room.

I tagged along behind the three of them; Kitty and I were foot soldiers marching, fighting the enemy – Red Indians – and doing what we were told by the commanders of the wooden fort, which the boys had built in a far part of the garden. When the boys didn't want to play with us, Kitty and I would read (I immediately fell in love with *The Jungle Book*), roam the garden or play charades. Granny taught us sewing and the basics of tapestry, and we were taken for walks every day.

The household at New Farm was fairly typical of well-to-do upper middle-class English families in the era before World War II. My grandparents were prominent in the Bromley community, highly respected, educated and conventional. They were devout parishioners at St Mark's Church of England, Bromley; the vicar came to lunch on Sundays after morning service. Granny hosted summer fetes in New Farm's gardens with stalls, games and delicious afternoon teas to raise money for church causes and the Dr Barnardo's homes.

For their day and means my grandparents were democratic employers. There had been nannies when their children were small, though the last had left when my Aunt Joy, the youngest, married. Now there were women of gentle background and different ages who came and went to look after the new generation of children at New Farm; they were known as the 'companion help', wore discreet clothes instead of a nanny's white uniform and were called 'Miss Surname'. Each was treated as one of the family and slept with us in the big children's bedroom, took us for walks, gave us our supper and put us to bed. I loved Miss Cotterell, who was young, affectionate and waiting to be eighteen to go to work in a bank; Miss Mellor, in contrast, was a thin, elderly, vinegary spinster who continually crackled brown paper in one hand – I disliked her intensely. Mollie Slin, universally known as Aunty Mo, was there from time to time. Mo was a devoted friend and ally of our Aunt Gay, and had originally been Kitty's nanny. She was young, dark and rather coarse looking, I thought, with the uninhibited snobbery of a seven-year-old! She favoured Kitty, which I resented, especially when she seemed not to care about Fred. Aunty Mo had many redeeming qualities, though; she was bubbly, funny and made us laugh. A few days after we'd arrived at New Farm I heard her singing as she ran upstairs and onto the landing: 'Tiptoe through the tulips, through the tulips . . . with me,' and 'Keep your sunny side up, up, keep your sunny side up . . .' The catchy songs were from the latest London musical hit; I can still hum those melodies, which always make me want to dance.

There were two live-in maids (one of whom was Queenie, whose name I so admired) who wore pastel-coloured uniforms and white caps in the morning to do the housework, then changed into their black dresses before lunch, which they served in the dining room. I learnt to help myself to vegetables with two silver tablespoons from a tureen or silver dish when it was handed to me on my left.

Miss Page was the head gardener in charge of every plant in the garden. She was a graduate of the famous horticultural college, Kew, and she wore their uniform, a green smock over fawn breeches and long leather boots. Miss Page had lunch and afternoon tea with us in the dining room. Bowler, the second gardener, carried out Miss Page's instructions, and the lanky gardener's 'boy' did the more menial outdoor jobs under Bowler's watchful eye. They all seemed to respect each other and understand the routine. Produce from the kitchen garden was picked by Miss Page in conference with Granny, then delivered to Bowler's wife, the cook, who looked like a storybook character: fat, comfortable, her ample body wrapped in an enveloping white apron. Mrs Bowler was accomplished and knew how to put delicious English food together. The Bowlers had a consumptive son who sadly died of tuberculosis while I was in England. There was also a chauffeur, Roberts, who drove my grandfather to his rubber factory in Bermondsey every morning and back to Bromley in the early evening.

One of my first memories of New Farm is of being taken to see Grandpa's new car: sleek, black and fast-looking, it was the latest of that year's design, though I don't recall the make. We climbed in carefully and sat with awe on orange pigskin leather upholstery, the smell of the pigskin a strong, clean, rather unpleasant odour which struck my senses sharply. I thought of the orange seats of Dad's car in Broome; a veneer of pindan dust made them that colour, and Dad always carefully dusted off the upholstery before climbing in to drive.

My grandfather, Frederick Henry Sprang, was a dapper man with thick silvery white hair. He had a serious countenance, though often his brown eyes twinkled with amusement behind his rimless glasses. He always wore a dark tailored suit, waist-coat and a gold watch, the gold chain falling across his stomach. I am told his business associates found him stern and steely. As a young man he had been slim and very handsome, though quite short, with dark brown hair and a drooping moustache, as was the fashion then. The miniature photograph I have of his head and shoulders, probably taken when he first met my grandmother, shows he had classic features, and he is looking upwards in a most soulful and typically Victorian manner.

Grandpa, always a brilliant and ambitious businessman, was chairman and owner, with a minor partner, of the firm C. E. Heinke & Co., submarine engineers and india-rubber manu-facturers. The firm was known worldwide (though my grandfather never thrust himself into the limelight, so kept the old Heinke name instead of giving it his) for exporting copper diving helmets, rubber hosepipes and complete diving gear to countries where pearl-diving was a thriving industry. Later I discovered that my grandfather was approached at one stage to make rubber contraceptives, and could have made an extra for-tune from producing them, but being the product of a strict Victorian upbringing, he considered making money from sex (in his eyes a sacred God-given activity of married love) to be immoral, so he turned down the opportunity.

His work made it essential for him to travel. My mother often told us of Grandpa's trips to the other side of the world – to Japan, the Dutch East Indies, Thursday Island, Perth and even Broome – through which he made many contacts. I remember meeting at New Farm two laughing Japanese girls wearing Western clothes, who were the daughters of a notable family connected with the Mikimoto Company, founders of the Japanese cultured-pearl industry and the first in the world to culture pearls. They were being educated in America and when they came to England on holiday, Granny and Grandpa were their guardians.

Grandpa had brought back from his latest trip some sou-
venirs that fascinated us. A particular favourite of mine was a
ceramic Japanese Buddha with a very tall forehead. I was promised, 'If you stroke his forehead it will bring you luck', a special
treat as the intricately shaped smiling icon was usually kept well
out of reach. There were also some long spears brought back
from Thursday Island, which adorned the downstairs lavatory.
This was a large room with a door of frosted coloured glass,
which opened out to the stone-paved terrace. The lavatory
itself was like a throne standing on a low square base of green
cement against one wall. Grandpa would go there with *The
Times* and stay for ages. Kitty and I would sometimes try to see
through the opaque glass, giggling and scampering off before
we were found out.

My grandfather was an inventor, too, and the British government of the day consulted him during World War I. He
invented the self-sealing rubber used on the fairings of early
fighter planes and, I was told, the collapsible rubber dinghy. He
was a philanthropist, and in 1914 invented and gave to Broome
its famous decompression chamber used to treat divers afflicted
with the bends. It was reported in 1915 that out of nine cases
of the bends treated by doctors in the Heinke Decompression
Chamber, only one diver died. (The chamber can still be seen
in Broome's Historical Museum.) Grandpa also gave the
Heinke Cup to Broome's annual Swimming and Regatta Club
Lugger Race.

Above all else, my grandfather was a kind and devoted family man, and though rarely demonstrative, he and Granny were

very close. I recall that every Armistice Day we would gather around the wireless to listen to the memorial service broadcast from London. Darling Granny always cried for the son she had lost in France, one of the very few occasions I saw her in tears, and Grandpa would stand behind her chair, hands lovingly on her shoulders. Mother and the aunts cried too. On another occasion, a family friend said to me, 'Your grandfather was recently asked to stand for Lord Mayor of London, but he said no, because he felt it was too big a load for your grandmother.'

While Grandpa was the head of the household at New Farm, it was my grandmother, Catherine, called Katie or Kitty, who ran it. She was a good-looking woman with a full, generous mouth, a steadfast gaze under straight eyebrows and greying hair coiled in a thick bun. She had met Grandpa at a musical evening which featured a choristers' group he had started up; he had once been a choirboy with a soaring soprano voice in Chester Cathedral. She thought he was a perceptive, idealistic young man, and extremely intelligent; he saw Katie's qualities of generosity, steadfastness and gentleness from the beginning and fell head over heels in love. He wooed her with persistence, and wrote numerous love letters to her in his elegant hand. Three years after his first letter they were married on 26 December 1887 at the St John Street Wesleyan Church, Chester. My grandmother kept his letters in their envelopes in a small maroon double-satin folder, the front exquisitely embroidered by her with his entwined initials 'FHS' in fine gold stitching, the back with a spray of wild roses. A still fragrant but fragile posy, dry and crumbling, the colours just distinguishable, gathered by my grandparents during their courtship at Swallow Falls on 14 April 1884, is carefully tucked away with the letters in a grey envelope, also in the satin folder. I treasure it today, almost one hundred and twenty years later.

Katie bore four children to Fred within a few years – Lily, my mother Doris, Billy and Grace (Gay). Many years later, Joyce was born. Granny suffered the loss of her eldest daughter, Lily, to pneumonia, and in the Great War, Billy, her only son. In spite of this she was always a strong, compassionate and spirited woman. Plagued by deafness and a crooked back, she handled her considerable household and her family astutely and efficiently and was highly respected by all. Both my grandparents were devoted to the royal family, and Queen Mary was my grandmother's role model. One day when Grandpa arrived home at four o'clock and sat down for afternoon tea, he was glowing with happiness, his face wreathed in smiles. 'The Duke of Kent visited us today, and asked me to take him for a tour of the factory,' he told us. He was overcome with joy and pride.

My grandparents, Catherine and Frederick Sprang,
on their Golden Wedding anniversary.

We took the smooth running of our lives for granted. Granny shouldered my mother's marriage problems diplomatically, and made sure of the wellbeing of all her beloved grandchildren. She gave us the opportunity to experience gracious living, fine standards, good manners, straight backs! She indulged Daisy and me with beautiful things – smocked Liberty dresses, shot taffeta and velvet frocks for parties, Jaegar dressing gowns, Mason Pearson hairbrushes and countless other luxuries. I remember in particular a sterling-silver-backed dressing-table set like the one Mother had in Broome: hand mirror, hairbrush, clothes brush and shoe-horn, but by these days no longer a button hook. Granny told me I'd be given a piece every birthday and Christmas until complete. I could choose the design, so it was art deco, very modern, angular and typical 1930s. Sadly it was left behind when my family had to evacuate Broome after it was bombed by the Japanese in 1942, but I still have a heart-shaped silver trinket box, embossed with flowers, that Granny gave me.

I was given music lessons by smiling little Miss Weedon on the ebony Bechstein grand piano in the drawing room, and Granny made sure I practised every day. Captain Glazebrook, an ex-army officer, came in the holidays to give Fred boxing, fencing and swimming lessons. In the absence of a swimming pool, the latter were performed lying on his stomach on a big upturned drum, doing breaststroke in the air. Kitty and I would take our turn on the drum, trying to imitate the odd movements, when the lesson was over. In Fred's case, at least, the lessons proved effective; he became a competent, confident swimmer able to surf the ferocious Broome breakers as well as languidly stroke through cooler English waters.

Granny made sure too that we knew the children's classics. After breakfast during the holidays, we sat down in the morning room. Mother read to us in her musical, cultured voice, several chapters at a time, from evergreen books such as *David Copperfield*, *The Water Babies*, *The Wind in the Willows*, Kipling's *Jungle Books* and collections of fairytales from Hans Christian Andersen and the Brothers Grimm. We shuddered at the cautionary tales and drawings in the German *Strewwelpeter* book.

We had A. A. Milne's Pooh books, a beautifully illustrated Greek mythology book, the Beatrix Potter books, the complete Flower Fairy book and countless others.

Granny was also an inveterate shopper. We all enjoyed excursions with her, and it's in my blood, so I'm an addict too. Aunty Mo would drive us to Bromley High Street in Granny's car, which was a big black box on wheels. It was roomy inside, had plenty of seating front and back with two let-down seats behind the driver where the smallest children sat and, hanging beside each back door silver vases, which sometimes held flowers. My mother sometimes drove, too, when Roberts taught her to be a proficient driver. When we returned to Broome she kept it up, driving around the town, though she preferred to avoid the rougher roads beyond the town's limits.

Once in Bromley, Granny would personally choose meat from the butcher and fish from the fishmonger. Then we'd launch ourselves into the more exciting shops and the real business of shopping would begin. We bought special material for my ballet costumes, and I always looked longingly into the windows of the famous shoe shop, Lilley & Skinner, once coveting a pair of pale green quilted-satin mules with little heels and short green floating ostrich feathers across the instep. Wonderful Granny, who loved shoes herself, had noted my yearnings and surprised me by giving those mules to me that Christmas. Thrilled, I clattered about in them upstairs in my dressing-gown, feeling grown-up and like a film star. We bought school shoes at Lilley & Skinner, too, and bronze leather or brocade party pumps with grosgrain rosettes on the toe. The pumps were secured over the instep by thin black criss-crossed elastic. In the shop we could peer through the broad funnel of the X-ray machine on top of a small platform where we stood to see if our toes were cramped – although I hated the idea of looking at bones – but the grown-ups were always anxious to check the fit. These curious machines disappeared later when it was realised that the X-rays might be harmful.

Besides the serious shopping, Woolworth's – where notices declared, 'Nothing over sixpence' – was a regular destination for Kitty and me. Out of my pocket money I bought a dazzling 'diamond' ring from their selection nearly every week and would promptly lose it while playing.

When the shopping was done, we'd have afternoon tea in a restaurant. We children adored hot generously buttered toast cut into fingers or triangles; we learnt good manners and did not take the most buttery piece from the inside when the plate was handed to us, only when it was closest. Sometimes I'd wonder if Tora was still burning the toast for Dad's afternoon tea, but rather thought he'd be able to manage the small amount required for Dad's solitary snack without too much trouble. It never occurred to me to wonder whether Dad might be missing us; certainly I was too busy exploring my new life to miss Broome, Dad or even my Australian friends.

I was soon familiar with the routine at New Farm. We were taken for walks every day, Daisy in her pram. In winter we wore black berets, overcoats and woollen gloves, gaiters and stout shoes; on wet days sou'westers, mackintoshes, galoshes or wellington boots. Outdoor clothes were kept in the long cloak-room next to the sink and the vase cupboards where Mother arranged flowers for the house. I loved the walks whatever the weather, especially when, as winter approached, there had been heavy frosts and the world was silver-white, each blade of grass, twisted branch, twig and stone sparkled like spun glass, and I jumped on shallow iced-over puddles to see them crack and splinter. On these days, the sun hung low, enormous and orange-red like a Chinese lantern in Broome. We sometimes went for interesting walks on Bromley Common with our nanny, especially when Kitty and Fred were home on holidays from boarding school. The Common seemed endless, and there was always something new and interesting to see. It was a wild area with many different kinds of beautiful trees, such as aspens with their quivering leaves. Animals scurried about – squirrels, rabbits, and once a fox. There were ponds and streams. In winter, trees with bare branches revealed dozens of huge rooks' nests; very sociable and endearing birds with a loud caw, it was a pleasure to hear them chattering to each other all at once.

Lunch was always a delight. I have never understood why people say English food is so poor; everything I ate at my grandmother's table was fresh, mouth-watering and cooked to perfection. Lemon barley water made fresh every day was poured into cut-glass tumblers. When in season there were baby potatoes in melted butter with mint leaves to help the digestion. Newly dug asparagus was cooked just right, crisp and buttery; there were luscious strawberries and thick cream. My favourite fruit forever afterwards were the fat raspberries, velvety in the mouth, sweetly juicy, uniquely fragrant, always served with cream, sometimes made into puddings, and occasionally combined with other berries in summer pudding. One of my most vivid and rapturous memories is Granny's Sunday trifle, the confection in a huge glass bowl covered in a white cloud of whipped cream, finished with carefully placed small pink crystallised rose petals and whole crystallised purple violets, which were marvellous to behold, aromatic and crunchy to bite on. Strewn among the candied flowers were silver cachous, tiny silver-coated sugar lollies like seed pearls. I have special thoughts, too, of the miniature cartons of cream, each holding about two tablespoons, placed at each setting on the breakfast table for pouring over cereal.

Afternoon tea was at four o'clock at the dining table, and gradually it became darker and darker outside as the days shortened. Tinker, like a small black panther, usually sat on the windowsill waiting for Grandpa – Roberts would come down the drive, headlights on, bringing him from the factory. Patch would be at Granny's feet, waiting for his tea. There was always a Dundee cake and a Madeira cake on the table, rock cakes, thin white triangles of bread and butter, milk for the children and tea in Spode teacups for the grown-ups. My favourite was home-made apricot jam on buttered bread, the nutty kernels scattered through the thick preserve. When everyone had finished, Granny poured the last of the tea from the silver teapot into the

Spode slop basin, stirred in milk and sugar and put it at her feet for eager Patch, who lapped up every drop.

On fine summer days we had afternoon tea on the side terrace outside the drawing room. A long, mossy green bank rose near the collapsible afternoon tea table, and as it was summer and informal, Kitty, Daisy and I delighted in rolling round and round down the bank, shrieking with laughter and staining our clothes . . . nobody stopped or scolded us. Fred would be off climbing trees with Roy or poring over his stamp collection, but could sometimes be enticed to play cricket, chasings or hide-and-seek with us. Any reserve between Fred and me had fallen away; we'd become friends.

Dinner was at eight, and was not attended by children until the age of twelve. The dressing chimes were tinkled by one of the maids at seven for everyone to change and then rung again at eight for dinner. I left England when I was eleven, and saw with envy my fifteen-year-old brother escort thirteen-year-old Kitty in to dinner when they were home from boarding school. After our baths Daisy and I ate our nourishing nursery meal upstairs and got ready for bed, difficult during long summer twilights while having to listen to the activities downstairs, or the grown-ups playing tennis, their laughter and the thud of the balls drifting enticingly up to our window.

One day soon after we arrived in England and Kitty and Fred had come home for school holidays, Aunty Mo said she'd take us to London for a treat. My brother and cousin had been before, but it would be a new adventure for me. It was a cool summer's day; Kitty and I wore suitable formal clothes, light wool tailored overcoats, white socks, lace-up shoes, kid gloves and small velour hats. Fred wore his school uniform, knee-pants, long socks, stout shoes, shirt and tie, school blazer and cap. We walked the short distance to Bromley Station, where we stood on the platform and waited. Suddenly there was a distant roar, which materialised into a huge, round, green engine, hissing and puffing vaporous steam from a silver stump on its top. Shiny steel rods moved quickly and smoothly up and down from silver wheels. I couldn't believe my eyes at such a sight! The engine slowed and stopped, still hissing, but more gently now. There were a number of polished wooden carriages attached to it. Aunty Mo opened the door of the nearest first-class one and we climbed inside and onto the seats. The train started up and rushed on, stopping now and again at stations while I looked eagerly out of my window. As we were crossing a bridge, I asked Aunty Mo, 'What is that creek?' 'The River Thames,' she answered, laughing.

Shortly the train pulled into Victoria Station, where there was a vast expanse of platforms with more steam trains coming and going or just standing silent, an enormously high glass ceiling and crowds of people hurrying to and fro. There were various shops and an electric sign displaying the word 'Buffet'. I was curious. 'What is "Buffet"?' I asked, pronouncing the word as it is spelt. 'Boofay,' corrected Aunty Mo. My English family was amused by my Australian idiom and accent, but they were quietly determined to train me to speak 'properly'. The grown-ups also did not approve of my Broome name, Buddy, and always called me Rosemary.

We walked onto the street to a bus stop and when a huge red and white square vehicle drew up we got on, clambering upstairs to sit on the top, which was open, with a wonderful view of London. Not long afterwards the smart new enclosed double-deckers were introduced, so upstairs passengers could shelter from rain and snow instead of having to put up umbrellas.

Another new experience for me was the tube. The steep moving stairways that descended to the platforms seemed to go on forever until we were deep underground. Every few minutes a round train with no engine exuded from the white-tiled circular tunnel, like toothpaste coming out of a tube, I thought, wondering if that was the reason for the name. When our train came we all got in, and in no time we were out again and going up more escalators. We went to Kensington Gardens and saw the legendary image of Peter Pan, the boy who never grew up, standing on top of his magical bronze pedestal, fairies and wild creatures carved all around it. Elegant white swans glided on the ponds, reminding me of Hans Christian Andersen's fairy-tale *The Ugly Duckling*. Then it was time for Aunty Mo to take us home, but she said we'd have afternoon tea first at the ABC restaurant opposite Victoria Station. We tucked into delicious food. My favourite meal from that moment on, I decided, would be poached egg on toast, followed by a cream horn.

These were fresh and scrumptious: crunchy melt-in-the-mouth pastry shaped like a spiral sheep's horn, the hollow generously stuffed full of fragrant raspberry jam at the top, then halfway down thick fresh cream right to the bottom.

It had been an eventful day for me, the hustle and bustle of London was wondrous and alluring. There was one last surprise in store. When I blew my nose back at New Farm, my handkerchief was black. Alarmed, I showed it to Mother, who said, 'It's only coal dust from the train, darling!' Suburban steam trains were beginning to be phased out and electric trains replaced them, to my disappointment.

London was a favourite destination of mine from then on, and we visited many times. On one occasion when we drove to London in Granny's car, we glimpsed a huge sparkling building in the distance. As we drew nearer we saw a long, high, arched glass roof over a glass structure and were told that this was the Crystal Palace. Queen Victoria's beloved husband, Prince Albert, had it built in the nineteenth century for public entertainment, and in 1851 he arranged for the world-famous Great Exhibition to be held there. One summer afternoon we went to an amazing circus under the enormous 'crystal' ceiling. Sunlight shone through onto a magnificent performance by animals, birds and showpeople, including a clown, breathtaking acrobats, a tightrope walker and a blonde woman in a pink tutu performing daring stunts effortlessly on horseback while her white steed tore around the arena. A few years later, back in Australia, I was shattered to hear that the Crystal Palace had burnt down in an uncontrollable fire. It was a glorious, unique piece of architecture.

It was a tradition for Granny to take us to London at Christmas for the pantomime, to the Lyceum or Colosseum for first-class productions. We saw *Where the Rainbow Ends*, *Puss in Boots* and *Cinderella*, where the handsome prince was in fact a beautiful actress with long stockinged legs, feet in high heels, and the clownish dame was a man! We would also view the elaborate festive decorations and buy presents in the big emporiums: Harrods, Harvey Nichols, Selfridges, Peter Jones. It was a long time before Australian shops showcased animated displays in their windows, but in London that first Christmas in 1929, a Harrods window entranced me and made me laugh with delight. It was a classroom full of schoolboy monkeys sitting at wooden desks. One monkey kept dipping the tail of the monkey boy in front of him into his inkwell; it came out each time stained with ink. Inside Harrods, we took a wrought-iron lift in which a driver turned a big wheel to take us up to another floor full of entertainment. There we sat on a vast Persian 'magic carpet' with small windows set into it here and there. A man told us to look through the nearest glass panel when he started to fly us over strange places . . . there was a buzzing noise and we were up and away, peering down at foreign lands unfolding below. Although we were firmly grounded, the trip was very real to me.

Another special festive occasion was the 'Lord Mayor's Show', an official welcome held to accompany the election of a new Lord Major of London. Close friends of my grandparents invited us all up to London to watch the procession from the vantage point of the fur factory they owned, as it was located right on the route of the parade. The grown-ups were thrilled by this offer, especially as it included a tour of the factory first, to look at skins being prepared for manufacture into various expensive items. All I can remember are the dried insides of animal hides stretched over flat surfaces and held in place by countless nails or sharp pins, a grim sight, I thought. They looked too much like the living creatures and 'people' like Ratty, Mole, Badger and Squirrel Nutkin, whom I loved, so I turned away.

I was soon distracted as the magnificent procession began to unfold below and we all crowded around a huge window to watch. The mayor, dressed in sumptuous regalia, sat in a glittering gilded coach drawn by bedecked horses, escorted by a liveried coachman perched above the carriage holding the reins, and outriders in traditional outfits. Clowns rollicked, jugglers performed, bands played, all amusing the crowds as His Worship passed by – I adored the wonderful historic pageantry.

Before we'd arrived in England, Granny had enrolled me at a small private preparatory school called Crofton, which was almost opposite New Farm. We began to shop for my school uniform straightaway: black lisle stockings, sturdy black shoes, dark serge box-pleated tunic, white Viyella shirt, school tie pinned with the Crofton badge, blazer, hat and gloves – very different from the skimpy cotton play clothes I'd worn to school in Broome. Dressing on dark bitterly cold winter mornings meant layers of woollen underclothes first. There was no comforting air-conditioning in the 1920s and '30s, only the dying embers of coal fires in the grates from the night before and, later, slow-burning combustion stoves. In bad weather I wore a mackintosh, wellington boots or galoshes, and a sou'wester hat. I walked to my welcoming little school up the long drive, crossed quiet Westmoreland Road, and went through Crofton's gate.

The owner–principal, Miss Skinner, was a tall thin lady with white hair swept into a bun on top of her head, who wore high-necked lacy blouses and elegant fitted skirts. I observed her closely every morning at roll-call, sitting on the small stage in front of a bow window, the assembly hall below, and admired the way the sun glittered on her gold fountain pen as she ticked off the names of the sixty or so boys and girls.

I went to Crofton aged seven and left in 1933 when I was eleven. The boarding school I was to attend later in Perth never gave me the confidence I gained while at Miss Skinner's; I think perhaps by then I had been uprooted too often and found it very difficult to settle. I learnt my lessons at Crofton with interest – even maths, which I came to loathe at boarding school. Geography was a favourite class. All our teachers were creatively devoted to their particular subject, and our geography mistress fired my imagination with stories of the Portuguese navigator Magellan, his expeditions to remote seas and to the Spice Islands, his cargoes of sparkling diamonds and other priceless jewels. In Australia I lost interest in geography, I think because we were taught in a dry way about winds and the produce of the continent – there was nothing to seize a vivid and romantic imagination.

I adored English and history, and have remained deeply interested in both subjects. I could write down the family trees of the kings and queens of England and loved poetry, acting and dressing up in school plays. I eventually acquired an English accent, pleasing my relatives and RADA-trained mother, who was always a stickler for pronunciation. I picked up acceptable youthful English idiom too, phrases like, 'I say, I've got a good wheeze,' or in other words, 'Listen, I've got a good idea.'

Sport was also a delight at Crofton. I ran and won, and leapt so well I became the champion high-jumper. My new enthusiasm for outdoor games, together with the ordered and tranquil life at New Farm surrounded by beauty, must have caused blossoming of mind and body, because in the soft dewy air my freckles disappeared, my skin grew fine and clear, my red-streaked hair thickened and curled. Mother brushed the top section back, tying it in a large becoming bow at the crown, and I lost my nervous squint. Relations would say as time passed, 'Rosemary looks just like Janet Gaynor.' She was a petite American film star, and I bore a strong facial resemblance to her.

These flattering remarks boosted a previously non-existent self-esteem. Looking in the mirror, I decided I had overcome my hopeless adoration of Roy Marchand and set my sights on a boy in my class, Ronald. Ronald was dark and good-looking. We'd gaze admiringly at one another, and that was all. A boy I disliked, Desmond, was not so reticent. He had a sniffly unwiped nose and came to school every morning with congealed breakfast egg dripping down the front of his jumper. Fortunately, he quickly realised I did not return his affection and promptly turned his attention to another girl.

Some of my closest friendships at Crofton were shared with a small group of girls, one of whom was our leader; she was a serious intelligent child with dark hair. Sometimes we all played at each other's houses after school; New Farm's garden was especially popular in fine weather. At one stage our leader suggested we form a secret society, so we met one afternoon in the round summerhouse in 'my' garden, sat on the curved wooden bench around the table, our chief with notebook and pencil in hand. We were to be druids and commune with the spirits of the garden. Our leader proposed we call ourselves 'The Wittenmegog Society', which sounded good to me, and I felt a thrill run through me. Sadly we left England not long afterwards and I missed the Wittenmegog and its imaginative founder.

Another fellow student at Crofton was an especially charming, pretty girl with red hair. Her name was Sheila Collett and she became a friend. She lived in a big Bromley house and we played together and went to each other's parties. Her father was a distinguished businessman; soon after we sailed for Australia he was knighted and elected Lord Mayor of London. Many years later, when reading the *Sydney Morning Herald* one day, I saw that a Miss Sheila Collett had arrived in Sydney to be companion–attendant to the daughter of the Governor of New South Wales. I would have loved to discover if the newly arrived English girl was the same Sheila Collett of Bromley. But my husband, John, and I were beginning our herb-growing business, Somerset Cottage, at the time and lived in a pretty little weatherboard cottage – not acceptable to Government House in the early 1960s, unless your background was well known, as mine was in Western Australia but not in Sydney. I did meet her at a luncheon some time later; however I was too young and insecure to break with the social mores of the day by asking, 'A long time ago I lived at New Farm in Bromley for four years, my name then was Rosemary Goldie, and I had a friend called Sheila Collett; I wonder if you are the same girl?'

At eight years old I began standing on my toes, even in shoes, so it was decided I should begin ballet classes after school at Crofton. Miss Hatfield, a retired dancer, was our teacher. Ballet shoes with small chunks of wood in the toes were bought and I began to learn an artistic skill I loved, so like many little girls my strong ambition was to become a professional ballerina when I grew up.

Miss Hatfield had high expectations for her pupils, was a wonderful mistress and prepared us well for exams. We learnt the French terms for ballet movements and practised assiduously at home and at the barre. Arms, hands and fingers had to be graceful and correct. Miss H drummed into us: 'When you are dancing SMILE, make it look easy and always SMILE . . .'

Together with other teachers of dance and various forms of artistic expression, Miss H arranged concerts for charities. We performed with other young people, bedecked in costumes provided by our families. Mine were made from beautiful materials – I was lucky to have a generous and interested grandmother. Eventually Miss H said it was time to go to London and compete in a renowned annual dancing competition. We practised fervently until the great day. Accompanied by Miss H, mothers and children travelled together by train to the vast hall where the competition was held. Miss H warned us: 'The judges are professionals and at these competitions children are chosen for pantomimes. They are always Cockneys with ambitious mothers and are extremely talented. Don't expect to win even a silver medal, but the experience will be unforgettable.' And it was!

In the large communal dressing room a tiny boy aged about six was dressed in miniature tails, white tie, top hat and was holding a cane . . . I thought he looked ridiculous. Was he Jack Buchanan? Fred Astaire? When his turn came to perform he was so brilliantly entertaining he won a medal.

Slightly chastened, I took to the stage. I thought my Piper Dance went down well, but clearly not well enough – to my chagrin, there was no mention from the judges after my spirited rendition. The dance served me well over many years, however, and could be trotted out if ever I was called upon to perform a party piece. Even now, its steps are indelibly imprinted in my brain and body.

In the June summer holidays each year, my grandparents hired a small private hotel for a month near the beach at Southwold, in Suffolk. Southwold was a quaint town, with uneven pavements and ancient little shops with mullioned windows. A town crier, dressed in red and black eighteenth-century clothes, would ring his brass bell and announce items of news twice a day, always preceded by the words, 'O-yez! O-yez! O-yez!'

Aunts, uncles, cousins and Aunty Mo all came on this annual holiday, and although the pebble beach, gentle waves and bracing water temperatures could not be compared with Broome's wonders, Southwold was loads of fun with its amusement pier and paddle steamer plying along the horizon. After breakfast every morning we would go down to the beach, where we had our own dressing shed in which to change into bathers and rubber slippers, and where we stored our buckets and spades. I would float in the shallows, or play on the shore with Kitty and Daisy. We'd go home for a late lunch and the ubiquitous afternoon rest, after which we'd often go for a drive to nearby Lowestoft or walk into Southwold for afternoon tea.

On wet days we visited centuries-old churches and chapels, which fascinated me. One had a 'priest's hole', a small back stairway with a peephole, which I was told was to facilitate escape for priests in centuries past when they were persecuted for taking mass to the underground Catholic faithful.

Kitty and I shared a bedroom on Southwold holidays, and got up to many pranks together, some her idea, some mine. Our room overlooked a house with a very tall chimney, which immediately presented itself as a challenge to me. I felt it was asking to have something thrown down it, just like the dummy clowns with the wide-open mouths at fun fairs. One day Kitty and I collected pebbles from the beach, stowed them away, and at dusk, after supper, we opened our window and took it in turns to throw a carefully aimed pebble down the gaping maw of the chimney. We were never successful, yet it looked so easy! Luckily for us, nobody from the targeted house complained about the rain of pebbles from next door.

I had met my Aunt Gay soon after our arrival in England. She had big blue-green eyes, an oval face, clear skin and thick dark hair. I knew she was creative and talented – my mother told me that she had a great gift for music and had gone to the Royal Academy to train. In a piano contest she had been awarded second place in all Britain. However, during the four years I lived at New Farm, I never heard Aunt Gay play one note on the Bechstein grand; events in her past must have stifled her great talent.

I never really liked Aunt Gay, though in later years my feelings changed and we exchanged long letters. I found her rather cold, calculating and self-centred, often finding fault, and she rarely spoke to me or showed me affection. Above all, I disliked the way she picked on my mother. There'd always been a rivalry between the sisters – Aunt Joy, my mother's youngest sister, told me later that they 'used to fight like cat and dog'. Mother had been the beautiful one in the family, and Gay, although pretty, was envious. Aunt Joy, however, was a favourite. With her dark hair and eyes she was very pretty, and she had an uncomplicated, happy nature and even temperament. She was a very practical person, making her own bread and fruit wine, and she grew her own vegetables and wildflowers. She was happily married and she and my uncle Fred, with their daughter Patricia, who was six months old when I arrived in England, lived on a farm in Canterbury, which we visited a few times. They were wonderfully hospitable people.

Aunt Gay could not have been more different. She was fascinated by the fashion world so Granny and Grandpa bought her a boutique in Tunbridge Wells, a market town. She would wear an outfit and then put it back on the rack (in pristine condition) and sell it. She always looked stylish and prided herself on being up to the minute. I remember well an ensemble she wore to a dance Granny and Grandpa gave at New Farm – a long 'Ginger Rogers' chiffon dress printed in shadowy greens with beige fur around the swirling hem and a jacket to match, also trimmed with fur. She and Mother came into the children's room where Daisy, Kitty and I were sitting up in bed, waiting to be kissed goodnight. Mother wore a colourful asymmetric chiffon frock, knee-length in front and ankle-length at the back, bought from Gay's shop.

Aunt Gay had a love affair we giggled about. Fred and Kitty had gone to dinner in London with the pair as a cover-up and all four had stayed in a hotel overnight. But Granny and Grandpa knew somehow, and gave Gay a long lecture behind closed doors.

Gay had married Kitty's father, Thomas Dodd, after her first love had been killed in France during World War I. Though it was not discussed, Gay's artistic nature rebelled against living with her farmer husband for long periods in the deep countryside, although he adored his petite wife. They did not divorce. While we were living in England, my grandfather tried to patch up the marriage, buying them in 1930 a charming mixed farm, Holland Farm at Langton Green, near Gay's shop in Tunbridge Wells and closer to New Farm and London than their original property.

This farm was to be one of the great joys of my life in England. I loved staying there with Kitty, who would spend only a week or two of the holidays with her parents because Gay preferred not to live in a country village for any length of time. Sometimes Mother, Fred and Daisy came to Holland Farm too, and somehow we all managed to squeeze into the tiny 'doll's house', which was very old and had the appealing individuality found in English cottages before the advent of councils and developers. I loved the way we opened a cupboard to reveal a staircase leading to a tiny landing, then took three steps up to Kitty's attic room. Three steps down again on the other side of the landing was a guest room, which opened onto Aunt Gay and Uncle Tom's room.

I loved, too, our journeys to Langton as I found driving anywhere in England a pleasure: the changing landscape of different seasons, smooth roads and changing scenery were a far cry from the bone-jarring dirt tracks through the endless pindan and remorseless heat of Broome. I was particularly taken with the ancient roadside stone markers which indicated the distance to the nearest town or village; in Western Australia distances were too vast ever to be signposted.

Most of the time I visited Kitty at Langton on my own and slept in a spare bed in my cousin's blue and white bedroom. Aunty Gay kept Granny's tradition of reading a classic children's book to us every morning after breakfast – a chapter a day – but after that the day was ours and we whiled away the hours roaming the farm and nearby countryside. One day we made our way into a large cornfield where the crop was ripe, the waving stalks so tall they were well over our heads. We had to feel our way to the very end, where we thankfully climbed over a stile into an apple orchard, in which the gnarled old trees overhung a sea of lilac lady's smock. At a later time when the corn crop had been harvested, the field became a tapestry of blue cornflowers, white daisies, scarlet poppies, mauve corncockle and leftover short stalks of corn-ears.

We often went into the dairy at the back of the house, where huge flat pans of fresh milk were placed on shelves for the cream to rise, the milk in different stages of setting. We'd select the one with the most cream on top, put in a finger, scoop up a big golden blob, quickly drop it into our mouths and swallow before anyone found us.

The cows were housed overnight in a long shed; after milking at dawn they walked to green meadows to graze all day and came home to be milked again in the late afternoon. I loved lying in bed at daybreak, half asleep, hearing the mellow ringing of the bells around their necks, their contented lowing. Each cow was named after a family member or friend. The first time I visited the farm one cow was stalled in the shed and Uncle Tom said, 'See, there's a new bull calf standing next to her, born yesterday.' The creamy-white calf looked at me with its big brown eyes. I looked back into the velvet depths and felt a loving kinship. I saw the skin on the calf's foreleg quiver and tried to make mine do the same. I begged Uncle Tom to name him for me, and he laughingly agreed to call him Goldie, as he pointed out that Rosemary would not be a suitable name for a young bull. I often thought of my little calf before going to sleep at New Farm.

Once when I was staying at Langton, Kitty had the idea that we should try smoking cigarettes. I was enthusiastic, aged about ten, Kitty twelve. There was a funeral going on in the village, the house was empty with the blinds down and we were alone in the downstairs sitting room. Kitty knew where the cigarettes and matches were, fetched them, put a cigarette in her mouth, offered me one and I did the same. She struck a match and lit both cigarettes. I inhaled deeply, suddenly choked, couldn't breathe and panicked. I ran upstairs to the bathroom, looked at my ghost-white face in the mirror, then ran downstairs again to my cousin, croaking, 'I'm dying!'

'No you're not,' Kitty breathed, enjoying her cigarette.

I calmed down eventually but didn't smoke a cigarette again for many years.

Early in 1933, Mother told us children that we would have to go back to Australia very soon. I loved travelling in ships, seeing new places and having new experiences, so wasn't too concerned. I didn't have the insight to know I had become an English girl; had absorbed into my soul the comfortable lifestyle, the loving routine and above all the glorious garden, which children were encouraged to roam in and enjoy as much as grown-ups. I could not foresee that the harshness of Broome, the blinding brightness and dramatic colours and noises, the daily grand shouting operas from my parents that I had experienced as a small child, would come as a shock. One night I woke to hear Mother crying in her room near mine, so I crept in and snuggled into bed beside her. 'What's the matter, Mummy?' Weeping quietly she said, 'Your father is writing long letters saying I must go back to Broome with you children, or he'll have you returned without me.'

Dad had visited England for eight weeks in 1931. I realised later that this must have been his attempt to take Mother and us children home to Broome. He was amiable and fitted in to life at New Farm, calling my grandparents Mater and Pater. I noticed Aunty Gay was suddenly affectionate to me and smiled a lot, fluttering her eyes at him. Aunty Mo acted in the same way, much to my astonishment. Dad obviously appealed to women – he could clearly be very charming. This was not the impression I usually got.

Granny, who'd suffered so with her bad back, always insisted that resident grandchildren lie on the drawing-room floor every morning so we'd grow up with straight backs, and we also walked around the room with books balanced on our heads. Dad reverted to type and drilled us like army troops as we walked: 'Forward march, attention!' Secretly aunts and uncles chuckled at this, they told me years later when I returned to England. Now I wonder whether the joke was on us: was Dad gently poking fun at a way of life he found too restrictive, too regimented?

Dad came to Southwold for our annual seaside holiday that year and told everyone how to eat shrimps with a squeeze of lemon and salt and pepper on small squares of buttered bread. The shrimps were minute compared to Barred Creek prawns, but there was no question, my father was an expert on seafood! Then one day Dad simply wasn't there anymore – he had returned to Broome, and his luggers and Tora, without his family.

As I lay close to Mother the night I heard her crying, buried memories of our life in Broome flashed through my mind in seconds. I was horrified by what she had said; remembered again the fireworks between my parents, the disturbing atmosphere around Dad when he was at home. I was too young to understand all the implications of our return to Australia that night, and soon fell asleep, but I didn't forget. Not long afterwards I suggested that our family of four – Mother, Fred, Daisy and I – should live together in a small house in Bromley near Granny and Grandpa, but Mother only said her parents had been distressed over her marriage in the first place and she couldn't bring the ugliness of legal battles into their tranquil lives in old age. 'I've made my bed and must lie on it!' were her words. Now I agree with her; Dad had a right to see his children.

During the next few months there was a lot of action, and a flurry of letters went to and from Australia. Around this time, Granny announced that she was taking Mother and me to a speech day at Farringtons. I had heard about this exclusive school because Aunty Joy had been educated there, and Queen Mary had been interested in the school and had visited it. I enjoyed the day and was impressed with the enormous portrait

In silk dresses and party pumps, this photo of me (left, aged nine) and Daisy (four) was taken at a Bromley studio.

of Queen Mary in the main hall. Not long afterwards at after-noon tea, Granny looked at me with her steady gaze and said, 'Rosemary, when your family goes back to Australia, would you like to stay in England and go to Farringtons?' At eleven I was unaware of the great compliment my grandmother was paying me, and all I could think of was being separated from Mother for a very long time. 'Oh! I couldn't leave Mummy, Granny,' I replied, and that was that; I didn't even thank her. The subject was never mentioned again.

Not long after this, I learnt that a dear friend of my parents, John Frewer, Bishop of the north-west, was advising Mother on Australian schools for Fred and me. He was on the council of Perth's Church of England boarding schools, Guildford Grammar and St Hilda's – the best, he said. I began to wonder how I would cope with being separated from Mother and everything I knew if I was sent to St Hilda's, but I managed to push the thoughts to the back of my mind most of the time. We were still in England, and I had the long voyage to Australia to look forward to.

I heard the grown-ups talking about ships and the best route to travel: through Suez or round the Cape? A liner was chosen for the shorter Suez trip. Then it was decided that Daisy's and my bad tonsils must be operated on before leaving England. After my earlier experience Granny didn't trust Australian doc-tors (the tonsils had grown again and were septic) so surgery was scheduled and the Suez option abandoned, because newly operated-upon throats would be susceptible to infection 'going through the tropical Red Sea'. In a similar vein, Granny forbade going to the Bromley cinema for fear we'd catch tuberculosis – a scourge at that time, with several local cases, and a crowd of people breathing the same air was considered the worst environment for contagious germs. Strangely, visiting big London theatres with plenty of space apparently didn't attract the same risk, and we went to Christmas pantomimes every year.

Finally, we were booked to sail around the Cape in Shaw, Savill & Albion Line's *Themistocles*, leaving Liverpool in the summer of 1933. Daisy and I entered a private Bromley nursing home, where a specialist surgeon operated, assisted by a reliable anaesthetist. Since my first tonsil operation I had dreaded having ether or chloroform masks suddenly clamped over my face – especially as it had happened again at New Farm when my sister and I had surgery for adenoid removal (safely carried out by our competent GP on the bathroom table, an acceptable procedure at the time!). After that I begged to be warned beforehand of any future procedures, and this time they told me. Later discussion with contempories revealed that it was common practice not to tell children what was about to happen – one friend remembers being told she was going to a party, before waking in hospital with her tonsils removed.

The black day, as Granny called it, finally arrived in June. My new green trunk was packed, Mother's, Daisy's, Fred's luggage was ready too. Grandpa must have left for the factory early, but he would have said an agonising goodbye to Mother. Uncle Harry, Granny's younger half-brother, had arranged to drive us to the boat-train leaving Euston Station in London. He'd park his car, come with us, see us safely on board the ship and wait and wave on the wharf until we sailed away.

The house at New Farm felt sombre and horribly quiet the day of our departure. Farewells were heartbreaking, Granny was crying, Mother and me too, my sister at six uncomprehending. Fifteen-year-old Fred was leaving his home of ten years, his school, the Kings School, Canterbury, and his 'Darby and Joan' as he called our grandparents. He was white-faced, but controlled. Eventually we were in the car, heavy luggage sent on ahead, and Uncle Harry motored down the long drive and into Westmoreland Road on our way to London, the train, and the ship that would take us to another life on the other side of the world. For me it was the end of a magical childhood, it was saying goodbye to Peter Pan's Neverland, to Christopher Robin and Pooh's enchanted forest and to Ratty and Mole's willow-hung riverbank.

As we drove into London the car entered a very wide road, probably Pall Mall, and we saw Buckingham Palace. Uncle Harry said suddenly to Mother, 'Look, Doris, they're changing the guard, there's time to stop and watch!' We were thrilled and got out of the car and gazed at this memorable sight. Soldiers wearing red coats, black trousers and high black bearskin busbies on their heads marched in formation back and forth outside the palace while the guards' band played. We watched until it was over, and Mother said, to keep our spirits up, 'Wasn't that lucky?'

Uncle Harry parked his car near Euston Station and we found our seats in the first-class carriage. Eventually the train began to move, picking up speed, and clack-clacked monotonously on its way to Liverpool. Mother sat close to her uncle; she must have been experiencing terrible sadness.

After rattling along for some time, I noticed a continual thudding noise in the next-door compartment and wondered what it was. I strolled into the corridor, looked in, and saw a man and a woman, a girl about my age and a smaller girl Daisy's size with blond curly hair. The youngster was sitting on a stationary bicycle pedalling like mad, which accounted for the thudding sounds. It was satisfying to know other children our age would be travelling with us.

Finally the boat-train pulled into Liverpool Station and we proceeded to *Themistocles*'s mooring. She was one of many ships lining the dock. We followed a steward to our three-bunk snuggery, a bibby cabin like *Ceramic*'s four years earlier. It was roomy with a passage down one side and a porthole at the end. We could lie in our bunks and watch the sea flow past, listening to the hiss and slap of the ocean against the ship's steel sides. Almost grown up, Fred had a cabin to himself. I asked Mother if I could go exploring, as it wasn't time for departure yet.

Themistocles was a two-class ship – we were travelling first – and second class was situated on lower decks. No trespassing was permitted for either section. I walked up a central series of broad stairs to the promenade deck and stood at the rail. *Themistocles* was not big: 11,250 tons with only one funnel. I noticed that the ship moored alongside her boasted layers of decks and several funnels, and I was envious. I turned and saw the older girl from the train standing next to me. Her name, she told me, was Mary Bennett. She and her family had arrived on the *Britannica* from America the day before and they were continuing on to Australia. 'Let's have a look around before the boat goes,' I suggested. We ran down the stairs to the dining saloon, which was on a low deck where a ship is more stable in rough weather. We shouldn't have been there of course, but the doors were open. I was intrigued to see laid out on the side tables plates holding tiny rounds of toast covered with what looked like shiny black seeds. 'Caviar,' explained a friendly steward. He quietly slipped Mary and me a morsel. I bit into the luscious roe and became an addict for life. Mother laughed later at my 'depraved taste', when I complained that the children's sitting never included caviar.

We hastened back to our cabins; *Themistocles* would be sailing soon. To my shame all I can remember of my feelings then are floods of excitement just thinking about the weeks of shipboard life that lay ahead, with my new friend for company. I joined the family and a bugle sounded, signalling that visitors should begin their farewells before going ashore. Faithful, loving Uncle Harry embraced Mother, me and Daisy and clasped

Fred's hand strongly. With encouraging words he left for the wharf while we stood at the rail with a crush of passengers. There were several deep-throated blasts from the funnel and *Themistocles* pulled away, though we kept looking down until Uncle Harry was just a speck in the distance.

We had a long six-week journey ahead of us, with only two ports of call – Tenerife and Cape Town – before *Themistocles* docked at Fremantle, 'the gateway to Australia', a rundown, shabby town then. The ship was fully booked, but there were no other passengers Mary's and my age, so we teamed up and were never lost for something to do. (To my delight, Mary turned out to be a day pupil at St Hilda's, though in the year above me.) A day after leaving Liverpool the ship entered the notoriously boisterous Bay of Biscay, the wide opening of the Atlantic stretching along parts of the Spanish and French coasts. Undaunted, my new friend and I played croquet on a heaving wooden deck as the ship pitched and rolled on turbulent deep furrows of green water. Down in the dining saloon portholes were screwed tightly shut as walls of waves crashed against the strong glass. Ships did not have stabilisers until a long time afterwards, but I was never seasick; being a Broome child and a seasoned sailor I liked the feeling of being at sea, learning to bend and let my body go with the movement. A ship's rhythmic rocking on the deep lulled me to sleep (like a steel womb, someone once told me), and I wasn't alarmed when stormy weather caused excessive tossing and things crashed and slid about.

As well as croquet, Mary and I played endless deck tennis, quoits and pinball games in the smoking room. At eleven o'clock every morning, tasty, nourishing beef tea brewed in the galley was served along with plain, salty ship's biscuits. Everyone turned up to drink the steaming restorative from white china cups. There were organised events: I still use a finely wrought sterling-silver napkin ring emblazoned with a gold and enamel crest that I won in an egg-and-spoon race. And Mary, my mother and I took part one evening in one of the shipboard concerts. I still have, as a memento of the event, a small folding program, complete with faded autographs, for an 'Impromptu Concert' held in the 'First Class Dining Saloon of TSS *Themistocles* commencing at 8.30 pm prompt on Thursday, July 6th, 1933'. I was to perform my Piper Dance, Mother was going to sing, and Mary would recite a poem. Luckily, my beautiful ballet costumes were in my cabin trunk, along with the sheets of accompaniment music. The piper's outfit was a flecked blue and mauve tunic with a jaunty Robin Hood cap to match, flesh-coloured tights and black ballet shoes.

We performers rehearsed many times before the concert, and

a Miss Rosettenstein played my piper tune on the piano. I practised every choreographed step taught by Miss Hatfield. Miss
Rosettenstein had become Mother's friend and had a reputation
for reading palms. On the night of the concert, after an early
dinner, she helped me dress in my outfit, so I felt it was an
opportunity to ask if I was going to be a ballerina. Taking my
hand palm-side up, she studied it for a few minutes, then disap-
pointingly said: 'No, you're going to be a writer.'

I was second on the program, so I waited out of sight for my
item, a nervous feeling in the pit of my stomach. I remembered
Mother saying a little stage fright was important because it
made you do your best. Miss Rosettenstein began playing my
music and, nerves forgotten, I pranced onto the cleared floor,
becoming an elfin sprite blowing soundlessly into my imaginary pipe, pointing my toes, bending my body this way and
that as I danced up hills and down dales, absorbed in the elemental world of the magical piper. Loud clapping greeted the
conclusion of the Piper Dance and there were even encores. I
bowed several times, glowing with pleasure.

A lot of passengers were disembarking at Cape Town, including a beautiful actress with green eyes and auburn hair. At the concert, she had recited a poem that sent a tingle down my spine: 'Overheard on a Saltmarsh' by Harold Monro. She and a young officer were attracted to each other, and Mary and I often spied on them sitting close together in secluded corners of the deck. There was another pretty, flirtatious woman you couldn't help but notice. One day she scandalised all the other female passengers, but not the men, when her floaty dress blew up over her head in a gust of wind on the top deck, revealing that she was wearing nothing at all from the waist down! She wasn't concerned and pulled her skirts down with a laugh.

The ship docked at Cape Town and we spent the warm sunny day sightseeing: I was fascinated by the graceful South African silver-leaved trees that seemed to mesh together in thick canopies on a drive up Table Mountain, and looked in awe at the Cecil Rhodes Memorial with its long wide steps guarded by eight black marble lions, four on each side. Later we went to a shop called Stevenson Mitchell's in the city centre, where I was allowed to choose a beautiful brooch which I adored and wore for years; it was a small carved ivory rose, each petal finely delineated, the central tight heart a delicate pink. This was considered suitable jewellery when I was young, along with short strands of polished coral, or pearls (Princesses Elizabeth and Margaret Rose wore them). I called mine 'my corals'. I also had a gold link bracelet with a hanging lock – 'real gold'.

Nearing the end of our voyage, Mother said to me one

evening, 'Come and look at the sunset. The sky is a magnificent colour when the sun is setting in Australia, quite different from anywhere else.' She'd spoken in a similar way about England before we left, about that country's expanses of soft greens. I remembered that driving back from Langton after my final visit to Holland Farm, she'd stopped the car and said, 'Come and look, Buddy.' We'd walked from the roadside to where the Weald of Kent rolled away in emerald downs, stretching a vast distance. She sighed sadly. 'Take it all in, darling, you won't see green hills and dales like this in Australia.' Further on through Sevenoaks we'd looked down at grey, turreted Knole – home of Vita Sackville-West – where once Mother had taken me inside for a guided tour. I'd gasped at everything, especially at King James's carved solid silver dressing table. But I didn't realise then that this was not all I was leaving behind. I could not have known that I would never see my darling grandparents, my Aunt Gay or New Farm again. Grandpa died during World War II, and Granny six months later. Both were in their eighties. New Farm had finally been sold to developers. Mother visited England again in the 1960s, but I was not to return for fifty years.

Close to Fremantle, I realised with a pang that the idyllic life I had known over the past five years was behind me now; I had to think about a completely different future. The night before we docked, I began to feel apprehensive.

Part IV

Return to Australia, 1933–40

Themistocles berthed at the Fremantle wharf on a sunny morning in August 1933. All passengers were on deck to watch, and welcoming friends and relatives stood in groups on the dock, waving. We'd packed the night before and said goodbye to fellow travellers who were departing at various ports further on: Adelaide, Melbourne, Sydney. Only a few of us were disembarking in Western Australia. The Bennetts and Goldies said we'd keep in touch; I knew I would see Mary again at St Hilda's.

Scanning the dock, I saw Dad standing on the wharf with close family friends the Margolins – Uncle Margy and Aunty Hilda, Daisy's godmother – who lived in Perth. My heart sank as I wondered if my father would still be the strict authoritarian I remembered from Broome, or easier to get on with as he had been during his visit to England two years earlier. We trooped down the gangway, greeted Dad, and squashed ourselves into Uncle Margy's crowded car.

I sat on Dad's knee and told him that my ambition was to be a ballerina. 'What!' he joked, 'a bally dancer!' I felt deflated – I wasn't prepared to be debunked. What a comedown! Arriving in Perth, Uncle Margy pulled up outside a big hotel, a typical Victorian establishment frequented by country people, but not the Esplanade this time. In the dining room, old friends, including Margot Field and her parents, who now lived in Perth, had congregated for a welcome-home lunch.

I enjoyed our ten-day stay there, and was especially happy to see Margot again, who had been allowed to spend the first night in the hotel with me. Dad spent most of his time discussing the war with Uncle Margy. Uncle Margy was a World

War I hero, a colonel of Russian Jewish descent, leader of a light-horse contingent and later Governor of Palestine, and my father worshipped him. Together they talked with great admiration of General Monash and General Birdwood, whom they had known well in the Middle East. Mother was not happy to be back, and almost immediately she and Dad began arguing as they had always done.

We caught up with other friends in Perth, notably Pam Gregory, whom I had not seen since I was six. It was a very happy reunion, though I felt immature in comparison to Pam who, at twelve, was already a tall, pretty girl enviably wearing high heels. While the adults chatted in Pam's grandparents' house, we preteens sat on rocks by the river and discussed our next meeting on the ship that would take us home to Broome for the holidays.

Another day, English friends of Pam's grandparents invited us to visit them on their yacht, which looked to me like a miniature liner, and was anchored nearby on the Swan River. It was a sleek, silver motorised vessel, and the couple were sailing her round the world. Indeed, they turned up in Broome at Christmas time. He was tall and slim, good-looking, but his wife was the interesting one. She was a very smart socialite and brave adventurer, with shiny black hair cut in a fashionable Eton crop. I can still see her thin boyish body in a long orange cocktail dress with a zip all the way down one side. She epitomised the era, always looking as if she were partying in an elegant Mayfair drawing room no matter what the surroundings. Six-year-old Daisy, however, was not impressed and with the innocence of youth referred to her as 'Mrs Man'.

In spite of these pleasant diversions, I was terribly anxious about starting boarding school. Fred and I were going to be the only pupils beginning at our respective schools, Guildford Grammar and St Hilda's, at mid-term, and worse still, Mother told me Broome was so far away from Perth that we would only be able to go home once a year – for the Christmas holidays. Fred wasn't worried; he'd attended boarding school from the age of six and knew exactly what to expect.

We were fitted out for our school uniforms, which were purchased from one of Perth's best shops, Bon Marché, and I discovered that St Hilda's clothing regulations were very strict – right down to brassieres, which I was not wearing then but hoped I soon would be. They were required to be a no-nonsense brand, Kestos, plain white cotton with no padding of any sort – not very romantic.

On the day mid-term break ended, Mother and Dad drove me up to the huge front door of St Hilda's stately building, where we were greeted by the English headmistress, Miss Catherine Small. She was in her late twenties, tall, dark and beautiful with dramatic eyes – one brown and the other green. I never knew which one to look at. Miss Small had a masters degree from Oxford, and though strict, was kind and greatly admired. She was both feminine and a feminist, always pushing her students to use their brains and their particular talents. She was far-sighted for her day; she had introduced the new Dalton Plan, which encouraged students to think and undertake research instead of relying only on what they were taught. But that was no comfort to me that first day. My parents told me afterwards that I looked such a little girl under my white panama hat as I went through the imposing double doors, which clanged shut behind me, 'like a prison,' Mother said.

From the first minute I found being at school an awful experience. As the only new pupil I attracted the censure of all eyes, as the girls stared at me and started to criticise me. It was torture. I was taken to a small six-bed dormitory for pre-teens. Cynthia James, Peggy Usher and two other girls slept there. Everyone was arriving back at school after the long weekend, so I stood uncomfortably in the school hall, the only stranger among the loud greetings. There were introductions and it was obvious that I was a curiosity with a plummy accent. I remember standing around a table with a crowd of laughing older girls and feeling simply miserable. I was soon to realise that nearly all the girls at the school had grown up together and spent the holidays larking about with their brothers from other Perth schools. I knew hardly anyone. I felt completely overwhelmed.

I did not settle in to boarding school happily, having to adopt not only a new curriculum but also different ways and manners of speech. The Perth landscape seemed strange and hostile after England's lush greens; it was intensely dry, the sparse spiky trees growing up out of fine white sand in a time before native plants came into fashion and were appreciated. I'd been spoilt by our long and carefree journey to Australia, and had imagined that school would be like an Angela Brazil novel – full of jolly friendships, secret midnight feasts, scrapes, hockey, the school madcap, the head girl nobody liked and then did in the end. My first three months were not like that at all.

I slept on a rock-hard bed in an open dormitory and my face was bitten red raw by mosquitoes delirious on new blood. The terrifying and cruel ex-army matron, clad head to toe in voluminous white and ironically referred to as 'Nursie', bore down on me every night and slapped citronella all over my face and eyes, causing them to hurt so much I cried. Once a week, on throat-paint nights, Nursie thrust long brushes dipped in some sticky antiseptic substance down our throats to prevent infections. She was never gentle.

I badly missed Mother. There were distractions, however; I went on with piano lessons and ballet, though the dancing school was well below the standard of Miss Hatfield's in England. Even for a little girl Australia seemed culturally backward after my experiences there; I gather now that perhaps that is the reason so many creative people flocked overseas to develop their talents. At any rate, I soon got bored tripping in line around the room with lots of other girls in lolly-pink frilly leotards – with no barre work or interesting new steps to learn – so I was allowed to give it up the following year.

As I learnt to adapt, I found there was much to appreciate about my life at St Hilda's. There was a splendid view overlooking the wide, blue Swan River, which wound its way to Fremantle and the sea, and was alive with elegant black swans with smart red beaks. When the moon was full it rose huge and daffodil-yellow over rippling water, making a molten gold path almost to our doorstep and reminding me of Broome's Stairway to the Moon. Granny wrote to me regularly from England, always enclosing with her letters a crisp new five-pound note.

It would be deposited into my pocket-money account at school, from which I'd be given a small amount each week.

And of course I made new friends, though in the first few days I'd been sure I never would. Fortunately, on the day that classes resumed, a slight, vivacious girl with dancing brown eyes and long pigtails came up to me and said, 'I'm Eve Illidge, Mary Bennett's friend, she told me about you.' I was tremendously relieved to have someone to talk to. Eve became a dear friend, and sixty years later we are still very close. Mary, too, was kind to me and sometimes invited me to stay for free weekends, even though she was in a higher form.

Very early on we were told the story behind the school's legendary namesake, St Hilda of Whitby, a story that inspired me. Hilda had been renowned for her learning and wisdom, and she was said to have rid the north of England of a plague of snakes. Ammonite fossils, an extinct group of marine molluscs, were found at Whitby, and became the symbol of St Hilda; the school crest on our blazer pockets depicted a shield decorated with three ammonites which looked to me like three curled-up worms. Above them was the school motto, *Domine Dirigi Nos*, meaning 'Lord Direct Us'.

Quite soon I made other friends, who I would be close to for the rest of my life, and was happy. Although I continued to dream of New Farm and wish I was there, I knew it could never be. Not long after we left England, Grandpa had sold his valuable acres to developers, finding it too difficult to keep up a house and garden now that the family had all left. He and Granny moved to a smaller house in Bromley. I found out later that the developers, in their contract of sale, had promised to save New Farm's five-hundred-year-old oak tree, but promptly cut it down once they took possession of the property. While I was pining for it, rows of houses were being built all over my magic garden – I'm glad now I wasn't there to see it.

At the end of the third term at St Hilda's I prepared to go home to Broome for the first time in almost five years. After the initial torturous months of boarding school I was looking forward to it immensely. Fred and I took the school ship for the first time, and to my delight Shirley Ogilvie and Pam Gregory were on board. Shirley, whose family now lived in Perth, was going to Broome to visit her grandmother, and Pam to spend the summer with Greg. Cynthia and Peggy from my dorm (though Peggy would leave St Hilda's for Perth College soon after) were also making the trip, travelling to their homes in Singapore.

That first trip home on the *Centaur* set the pattern for all the school ships that followed for Fred and me: we played the usual deck games, cards, snakes and ladders, ludo. I discovered comics and creaming sodas too, but the highlight was a fancy-dress party. I swapped my colourful dancing outfit, a Hungarian peasant costume with a pretty beribboned flowered headdress, for Cynthia's exotic green silk Japanese kimono and strappy little mules with heels. I didn't realise until later that every Singapore girl owned this unfamiliar version of dressing-gown and slippers. Clever Pam went as Gandhi, wearing a white sheet draped over her shoulders, a pair of rimless glasses and her straight brown hair pulled down in straggly wisps. She sat cross-legged on the deck with a handful of raisins – there was no mistaking who she was and she deservedly won first prize. To my irritation Cynthia won second prize in my Hungarian outfit, but when big heart-throb David Gibbings put his arm around me and said how sweet I was to lend it, I blushed, managed to smile in a generous kind of way and felt better.

I was very shy at eleven; I didn't know what to say to boys and flushed red if they talked to me. Another blow to my self-esteem had been my changed appearance. I looked in the mirror one day and discovered that my face was once again powdered with freckles, which had sprung up under the Australian sun; my nose had grown as well, and I was covered in 'puppy fat'. Cynthia, though a year younger than me, was sophisticated and at ease with all the boys, perhaps due to her very social Singapore upbringing. She had blonde hair, blue eyes, and was once described as 'a young Ginger Rogers'. Peggy was a year older than me and had been going back and forth to school for years, so she knew the ropes. She was very pretty, with big green eyes and full red lips. Fred, who considered himself an expert in judging girls, would say, 'I'm fascinated with Peggy's pouty lower lip.'

We went ashore at several ports. Geraldton was the most civilised – a small version of Perth – but to my dismay the towns became more and more basic the further north we went. Port Hedland was the last stop before Broome, our journey nearly over. When the gangway was in place we trooped down in groups and strolled around the ugliest collection of buildings I'd ever seen. The place was eerily silent and empty of people in the midday heat. The fierce sun was blazing down on corrugated iron and there wasn't a spot of greenery anywhere; we could hardly wait to walk back to the comfort of our temporary home. At dusk the steamer was invaded by local youths in dreadful bell-bottomed trousers, their gelled hair slicked into greasy quiffs. They swept around the decks as if they owned them, throwing us contemptuous looks. We glared back with equal disdain, referring to them unkindly as 'the town toughs'. Everyone was allowed to board ships when they were in port in those days; security as we know it now did not exist.

After breakfast the following morning we lined the rails as *Centaur* approached our destination, trying to see the speck that was the wooden jetty in the distance, and as we drew closer, we could make out the faces of the people standing there. Fred and I spotted Mother in a bright dress and straw hat and Dad beside her in a tropical white suit. Little Daisy was excitedly jumping up and down. Before the gangway was in place I took in the scene in front of me and memories began to surface. There was the half-mile wooden jetty with its single railway line, and the funny little steam train. I remembered that when it was ready to go it would let out gasps of steam, shrill whistles, and then jolt into motion, clattering along its meandering route to town. There was the cattle race clinging to one side of the jetty; I'd seen station hands from outlying properties prodding bellowing animals along into a vessel's hold when the ship was headed to the meatworks at Wyndham. The sweltering heat and the smell of mangrove mud from the shore overwhelmed me. I looked anew at the blinding colours; the turquoise waters of Roebuck Bay, the blood-red rocky land and green mangrove-fringed harbour above sharply white beaches, the sun's heat and glare magnifying the extraordinary scene.

And then we were off, shouting 'Happy Christmas!' to those still on board and greeting the family with joyful shrieks and hugs all round. Our trunks were loaded into the goods trucks; they'd be delivered later. There were old friends everywhere. Greg was there to meet Pam, and Shirley's grandmother for Shirley; many more welcomed Fred and me back. We walked along the jetty to the car. Fred and I climbed into the dicky seat and we drove to our house on Walcott Street where dear old Tora was waiting. He was thrilled to see us, especially Fred – his favourite – who hadn't been home in ten years. For his part, Fred was delighted to be back. Like most men, he loved the freedom of the pearling town.

Treading up the steps into the house I started to recognise my home even though it seemed I had been away for so long. The latticed verandahs, the hatstand hung with a multitude of hats. There was the kitchen with its four-burner kerosene stove and wooden sink and Tora's room leading off the cluttered back verandah. The outside lavatory was a renewed shock – I'd become used to the civilisation of the indoor lavatories in England and in Perth.

We sat down for lunch at the new teak table Dad's carpenter had made, along with eight attractive teak chairs. We ate our seafood as the overhead fan stirred the insect-laden air and my homesickness for New Farm bubbled up inside me. Would La Bonbonnière be my home for evermore? I had so looked forward to my return and seeing Mother; now I felt like I had washed ashore at the end of the world.

The following morning Dad said he would take Fred and me down to his camp on the foreshore of the creek. A few of the crew were still there to service the luggers for next season's pearl-shell fishing, though as it was lay-up many had gone home to Asia. Fresh crews of Koepangers, Filipinos, Malays, Japanese and Chinese would arrive by ship in the new year and sign on with a master pearler for the season, receiving a year's payment in advance.

Fred and I climbed into the 'Greengage' with Dad and we drove along the red roads, past rambling bungalows and small cottages with green lawns. Japtown looked no different from my hazy memories; the shabby, corrugated-iron buildings blazed under the fiery sun. We passed the Sun Picture Theatre on our left and bumped down a long track surrounded by mangroves until we reached the camp. Several black-hulled luggers were drawn up onto the glistening grey mud and sat in watery trenches. The crew greeted us from their thatched shelter, where they were having a smoko. Dad began to rouse them, speaking in pidgin English: 'Time you boys start again, get ready sink boats full tide, drown cockroaches, rats.' Everyone in Broome adopted pidgin English when talking to people of other races; it was quite acceptable and Fred and I both recalled speaking this way to Tora and our maids and nannies when we were very young. Greg was one of the few pearlers fluent in Malay, which most crew spoke. Perhaps this is one of the reasons he was such a successful pearler.

Dad introduced us to the crew by our first names, but any intimacy ended there. I felt awkward, having no understanding of their backgrounds and nothing in common with them. I did recognise dear old Toshi, the carpenter, and Ah Wong, the gentle Chinese cook on Dad's main lugger, *Rosef*, and so did Fred, even after all those years away. Dad inspected the camp thoroughly and gave some more instructions to the men. Then I noticed two slick black-haired Filipinos ogling me and, outraged, I flounced back to the car, banging the door shut, and stared stonily down at my feet. My white sandshoes had been stained pink by the fine dust. Gloomily I remembered how iron roofs in Broome were often coloured in different shades of red as the salty air blew Kimberley soil onto them, and eventually the crust deepened to apricot and dark orange until the iron

Dad at sea.

Dad and his crew at Dad's
Dampier Creek camp.

rusted away completely and collapsed. My homecoming was going from bad to worse.

I was unprepared for the shock of a Christmas in Broome. We gathered around our tree on Christmas morning – a scraggy, drooping native sapling harvested from the scrubby bush across the road, propped up in a kerosene tin swathed in bright green crepe paper. Mother had done her best to decorate it with shiny baubles and tinsel. Piled underneath were presents wrapped in snowy holly-strewn paper, but overcome by nostalgia for the Christmases I had known in England I had to try hard not to cry.

All I could think of was the snug cosiness of Christmas there, the cheerful warmth of leaping flames in the fireplaces while the weather outside was freezing. Four days before Christmas Bowler would cut long, thick, leafy sprays of pine which we wound around the banisters and made into a bushy archway in the big hall. We'd add sprigs of holly alight with red berries from the tree that grew outside the dining-room window. A bunch of mistletoe was hung and aunts and uncles kissed and giggled under it, not all belonging to each other! We danced around the Christmas tree, a big silver star shining at the top, sang carols and relished a wonderful midday Christmas dinner with all the trimmings. I missed those rituals.

But by mid-morning that Broome Christmas Day, after the service at our small weatherboard church, and the tree episode, everything changed for the better. Crowded into the 'Green-gage', we rocked along the tyre-tracks to Cable Beach and met up with the Gregorys, McDaniels, Normans, Males, Morgans and many others. Everyone surfed the huge monsoonal waves that were crashing into the sand except me; I cautiously splashed about close to the shore.

After our swim we drove in convoy to the Gregorys' for drinks and watermelon, and then dispersed for Christmas lunch. Mother and Tora had prepared a traditional European Christmas dinner, which Tora had finished cooking while we were at the beach. He'd set the table formally, including red and green crackers. So full afterwards I felt I could burst, I slept soundly at siesta time.

In the evening everyone met up again for more fun and greetings, and this continued in much the same way until New Year. I recalled the Broome ritual of my early childhood of storming into one another's houses at midnight, high-stepping along verandahs, quaffing drinks and gathering friends as we went from house to house. Then we'd end up at one house, link arms and sing 'Auld Lang Syne'. I realised I was beginning to enjoy my outback Christmas.

In the weeks that followed, and during the other Christmas holidays over the next five years, I spent as much time as I could with my friends. We'd walk to Town Beach, and if we could coax someone into driving us we'd go to deserted Cable Beach or Riddell Beach. (There were no camels in Broome in my day, and certainly not on pristine Cable Beach.)

I remember Riddell Beach as everyone's favourite playground, and days of fun there with my friends. We'd drive on the tyre-tracks grandly called Gantheaume Point Road until we came to the plateau of red earth and crazy outcrops of vivid sandstone on the cliff's edge; the rocks going all the way down to the blood-orange beach, their weird shapes caused by the wind. The fierce red earth always reminded me of Dad in a rage – red face, red hair, a bonfire. I'd laugh!

When the cars were parked at the top of Riddell, we'd scramble over large boulders to the beach. If the tide was in we'd plunge and frolic in jade-green sea-caverns open to the sky; some pools, as big as rooms, led into others through jagged archways. At low tide, we'd watch the boys play with hermit crabs; squadrons of the small crustaceans lived at Riddell. To me, hermits were crab-comedians, looking comical when they scuttled on the sand between rocks, each wearing a different kind of shell – the discarded homes of molluscs – on their backs, too big or too small, and worn at an angle like a French beret. We'd crouch in a circle and watch the boys carefully pull some of the soft creatures out of their homes and line up the shells; the naked crabs searching until they found their original covering, then crawling back inside without effort.

When we grew tired of the hermits, we'd swarm over the rocks picking up beautiful shells, cherishing the small, rare operculums whose inhabitants shut their round hard doorways of celestial-blue or rose-pink when we touched them. Pam was collecting enough for a rare and individual bracelet Greg had promised to have made up for her. Brightly coloured tropical fish, left behind by the sea, darted and flashed in tiny lagoons; scurrying crabs hid under ledges; starfish curled up when prodded.

I'd stop to look at the giant clams in their shallow ponds, scalloped hinged shells closed, a few gaping wide waiting to catch an unwary foot. We'd keep watchful eyes open for the beautiful but deadly fish-eating cone shell. The long spectacular-looking cone houses a vicious creature with a lethal sting as venomous as a sea snake's, which can shoot out its toxic bite anywhere along the wide opening of the shell. We were told that large cone shells were common in our tropical north, and quite different from the small and harmless worm-eating cones, but I don't remember ever seeing the dangerous ones.

We sometimes found young trochus shells washed onto the shore, a spiral pyramid shape, speckled and striped in coral colours as if an artist had painted the pattern onto the pastel pink and beige background. Trochus shells grow to over thirty centimetres in height, and become broad and wide at the base. When the shell's crust is filed away, a mother-of-pearl sheen is revealed, and although the glow is not as radiant or pure as the pearl-oyster's nacre, trochus has its uses in commerce, and has been gathered by pearlers along with pearl-shell. When the small trochus I had at home was turned upside-down I could see the pearly gleam at its curlicue entrance. I'd hold the opening to my ear, as Mother had taught me, and hear the susurration of the sea breaking on the vast Broome beaches.

At Riddell Beach we remembered Captain John Riddell's grim fate at the hands of mutineers. He was a pearler, and uncle of a friend and fellow pearler, Claude Hawkes. He intended to fish the pearl-shell beds of Broome and the Ninety-Mile Beach. After he had lost luggers in a cyclone, Riddell bought a new brigantine, the *Ethel*, and signed on a crew of Malays, Manilamen and a Chinese cook. One night at full moon while *Ethel* was anchored off the beach that now bears Riddell's name, some of the crew sharpened their long knives and murdered the skipper, his son Jack and the white mate who were asleep in their bunks. The mutineers terrorised and cut the throats of any men who resisted, and took over the brig. Unable to navigate, the pirates lost their way, drifted until land was sighted, then scuttled the *Ethel*. They rowed for shore in dinghies with the last of the men and pretended to be survivors of shipwreck. The Chinese cook, who was nearly murdered himself, whispered the truth to authorities; the criminals were apprehended, tried and hanged at Fremantle jail.

Some said the Chinese cook was John Chi, well-known Broome identity, and owner of the Long Soup Kitchen in Japtown's John Chi Lane. We often went to his corrugated-iron cafe and ate delicious Asian food. John Chi's speciality was long soup, a fragrant spicy liquid thick with smooth, flat noodles, mysterious, aromatic morsels and crunchy Chinese vegetables. Deep bowls of the combination would be filled to the brim, a meal in itself. John Chi would smile his gentle smile as he placed the food, chopsticks and painted pottery spoons in front of us. It felt as if we were in Hong Kong or Shanghai, the air subtly scented with burning incense and wafts of exotic cooking. The gramophone in the back room played strange Chinese love songs, the shrill voices reverberating against the hot unlined iron walls of the cafe. I longed to ask John Chi about Captain Riddell's *Ethel* and the murdering pirates, but knew he would only smile inscrutably, sigh, and say he '. . . not know'.

The length and breadth of Cable Beach made it ideal for cricket. Fred was always captain; he set up the wickets and shouted orders. I had no ball sense and was a bad fielder. 'You let the ball slip through your fingers, face-ache!' Fred would scold loudly. One day, red-faced and feeling stupid in front of the others, I ran after the ball as it rolled towards the lapping waves, and on picking it up came face to face with a deadly sea snake reclining half in and half out of the water. It lifted its evil-looking head, staring at me with baleful eyes. I screamed, ball in hand, and ran for my life before it could strike at me.

Barred Creek was a favourite spot, though too distant and dangerous a trek for us to undertake by ourselves. Dad loved going there and one day he said he'd take the family and one of my friends. I managed to persuade him to squeeze in one extra so the twins, Sheila and Flora, came on this expedition. Mother packed a picnic and Dad drove us through dense grizzled bush, the usual mobs of kangaroos suddenly and silently leaping out to streak along beside us like misty phantoms until in unison they melted back into the scrub. Daisy sat in front with Mother and

Dad, and Sheila, Flora and I squeezed into the dicky seat outside at the back of the car, taking it in turns to open and close the gates so we could pass through. We sang the latest hit as we careered along: 'You go home and get your scanties, I'll go home and get my panties, and away we'll go, we'll shuffle off to Buffalo.' I had learnt it when I arrived at St Hilda's – everyone had been singing it – nevertheless we felt very daring. Eventually Dad pulled up at a large and decrepit corrugated-iron shed. We all went in; around the unlined walls were rows of raw timber shelves crowded with ancient dented tins of food, their faded labels peeling off, looking extremely unappetising. The place was a well-known stop for passing itinerants or for Broome loners who came out fishing for the large sweet-fleshed barramundi, huge crabs, succulent crayfish and prawns. The shelves looked as if they were restocked only once in a blue moon.

Being a seadog conversant with tides, Dad planned our arrival at Barred Creek for when the sea had retreated and it was safe for us to walk along the oozy, mangrove-lined mud to where it met the ocean. We took our things from the car, then in a tight group squelched along in sandshoes, scattering armies of scurrying crabs, to where blinding white sandhills and sparkling waters beckoned. Dad remained vigilant, watching for stray crocodiles.

On top of a high, windswept sandhill was another tin hut, this one clean and glinting in the bright sun. It belonged to a friend, and Broome couples would sometimes rent it for a few days, leaving their children at home with friends. The twins and I put on our bathers and ran down to the vast, empty beach, not a soul in sight, then, looking around to make sure, we stripped off to bare skin and plunged into the pristine gentle swell. The ocean felt like cold soda water, squirting sharp bubbles onto our naked bodies.

At mid-afternoon, our picnic devoured, Dad said we must go before the tide came in or we'd be cut off until the next day. We didn't dawdle along the creek bed, where trickles of returning ocean began following us, but climbed quickly up the low mud bank to dry ground. Driving through the late afternoon back to Broome, our skin tingled from the sun and the effervescent seawater.

The holidays drew to an end and we packed our trunks for the trip back to Perth. The awful knowledge that I wouldn't see Mother again till next Christmas made my heart sink, and Fred felt the same. It must have been heartbreaking for our mother, but she set an example, smiling all the time, never crying. She wanted her children to have a good education at whatever cost to her feelings.

On the dreaded day, *Centaur* swept in from the horizon, in a hurry to pick us up as the tide would soon begin its outward turn. Our friends already on board crowded along the ship's railings and began singing, 'Oh Rosemarie I love you,' to my acute embarrassment. I climbed aboard, and after a painful farewell to Mother, Daisy and Dad, I started to sob, as did the boy next to me. Fred had disappeared, and I was only aware of my own desolation. As the boat pulled away I wondered how I would survive, but my friends soon surrounded me, laughing and joking, and led me into the hectic happy life I remembered from the last trip.

There was a new boy on board: a very handsome fourteen-year-old with an Indian mother and an English father. All the girls developed a 'pash' on him, including me, especially when he stood and gazed intently at me one morning with his black eyes. But to my disappointment his favourite turned out to be a slightly older flirtatious St Hilda's girl called Mocky. I did learn, however, that Harold Gibson, Peggy Usher's cousin, had been singing my praises after the last trip, and we were both teased (hence the chorus of singing when the boat had pulled in at Broome), but sadly I didn't feel the same way towards him.

Just outside Fremantle, a doctor came on board to inspect our throats and outstretched arms for signs of tropical disease. All clear, we glided towards the dreary wharves and I was over-come with the bleak reality of another nine to ten months away from home. At least I was no longer a friendless new girl, and as school began I realised it was not the miserable experience it had been the year before.

New accommodation for the juniors had been completed during the holidays, a separate building named Margaret

House. There were more of us now, and we slept on a long open verandah – though still on hard beds. We had a big communal bathroom with shower stalls and a few bathtubs, and a common room where we could play the piano, write letters and play games. The dreaded Nursie was still with us, and she ruled over Margaret House with her usual rod of iron. Every day at 6 am she plunged with enjoyment into an icy cold bath, winter and summer; we girls took cold showers every morning, dodging under and out swiftly, and soaked with pleasure in a hot bath one evening per week.

After showering we dressed in our uniforms, dove-grey and sky-blue with gold trimmings. We wore tailored grey suits, grey lisle stockings, grey hats and gloves on formal occasions or for going into town, and white dresses, gloves and panama hats to church in Cottesloe on Sunday and for Speech Day. One day an older girl got into the small bus that stopped outside the school gates on its way to Perth. She had a mature boyfriend, and to my fascination she took her hat off, removed the school band, pinched fashionable creases into the felt, put it on again and cocked it to one side, then fished a lipstick out of her handbag and plastered it over her lips. She suddenly looked eighteen.

With morning ablutions out of the way we trooped over to the main building and ate breakfast at the juniors' table in the dining room, with Nursie sitting at the head. She never tired of talking about her favourite girl, who was a senior, two or three years older than most of us. She was sweet, pretty, mild and had impeccable manners. She practised the piano faithfully and was such a model of goodness that Nursie would repeat constantly, 'You must all try to be like Z.' Z's widowed mother was a rich and beautiful woman. What Nursie didn't know was that Z's mother kept a string of live-in lovers, one of whom she threw out at one stage. This fellow took his revenge by becoming an 'uncle' to Z, taking her out for the day at weekends, the unsuspecting staff happy that an older family friend should pick up the teenager. The 'uncle' would drive Z to his flat, his perverted intention to seduce the fourteen-year-old, which he did. The affair went on for the rest of Z's schooldays. This sort of behaviour was probably as common then as it is now, but no-one was aware of it at the time. Z told me the story in later years after we'd left school – she still loved the man.

After breakfast we would assemble in the big hall at the main school, where our headmistress would say prayers while we stood in orderly rows, daygirls and boarders together. Classes followed until recess, and then there were more classes until lunchtime. Mid-afternoon, we had a bread and jam break, which we hungry boarders eagerly awaited. Two seniors collected and carried out a huge plate piled high with white bread, cut into halves and spread thickly with jam – no butter. We descended upon them like animals at feeding time. A second piece was not allowed – even if it had been, there was never any left.

At the end of the day we could do as we liked for a while – homework, or write to parents, which was obligatory once a week. Then we changed into pretty dresses, ate our evening meal, and assembled once more in the hall for evening prayers.

We all admired Miss Small, who always looked glamorous in her elegant evening clothes. 'Doesn't Kate look divine?' we'd whisper. After prayers we'd disperse, the older girls going off to dance to the latest hit records played on a wind-up gramophone, taking it in turns to be the boy, the juniors heading for the common room in Margaret House.

I was not an all-round scholar, but loved English, art and history, often coming top in those subjects, and I liked, with middling results, French, German and biology in the lab. I loathed anything to do with mathematics: algebra, geometry, the awful set square. I was unable to work up an interest in geography since the syllabus concentrated only on Australia, so gave it up at the first opportunity. However unorthodox or unfashionable my choice of subjects, Miss Small enthusiastically encouraged all her scholars' gifts, and she, my art teacher, and Miss Lane, my English teacher, had faith in me and I shall always remember them fondly. (Miss Small later came to my wedding and gave me a full watercolour painting kit with brushes, pencils, several kinds of paper and painting blocks. Miss Lane presented me with *The Albatross Book of Living Verse*, which is still intact, though now well-thumbed.)

In my later years at St Hilda's a new block went up on one side of the quadrangle; downstairs was a domestic science room, upstairs the handicraft and art room. A good friend, Jeannie Drake-Brockman, and I opted to do domestic science simply so we could eat the food we'd prepared. We shared the cooking, and when we made Christmas cake, ours was the smallest because we'd eaten most of the ingredients while preparing it –

boarders were ravenously hungry all the time, though we were certainly not underfed.

We were allowed to go out on visits on the weekends, and I would spend a day each term with one of my close friends, Julia Drake-Brockman (there were various branches of the Drake-Brockmans in Western Australia: my other friend Jeannie Drake-Brockman's clan were landowners 'down south'). Julia's parents, Henrietta and Geoffrey, were close friends of Mother and Dad's. Henrietta was a beautiful and adventurous blonde who had once gone out on one of Dad's luggers for the day, had donned full diving gear and was lowered over the side to see for herself what it was like on the ocean floor. She also wrote a book, among many others, about the sunken Dutch vessel *Batavia*, diving in appropriate gear to investigate the wreck. Life was very formal at their house; we children would join the grown-ups for afternoon tea.

Judith Drake-Brockman, a champion swimmer, and her younger sister June were friends too, and still are today.

Aunty Hilda and Uncle Margy Margolin were wonderful, taking Fred and me for interesting drives and marvellous suppers at their house before dropping us back at school. A highlight for me came in October 1934, when the Duke of Gloucester arrived in Australia on the HMS *Essex* for a visit. There was a great fuss in Perth about the occasion, but I was especially excited as a relative of Mother's, John Bridgewater, was a naval officer on board the *Essex*, and the Margolins arranged to take Fred and me to meet the ship at Fremantle and take John out for the day. I imagined he'd be in full naval uniform draped in gold braid. However when John stepped off the ship, I was extremely disappointed to see that he was 'in mufti', wearing a smart fawn suit – no uniform, no gold braid! Nevertheless he was a charming man and we all had a happy day together.

I'd often think about my family in Broome, and especially about my mother. I worried that she might have another baby and die, as she nearly did when Daisy was born. I grew to be rather nostalgic about Broome itself, and in spite of my initial shock about its isolation and roughness in comparison with England, I realised how much I enjoyed being there with all my friends when we went back for the holidays.

In March 1935, not long after I'd returned to school from my second Christmas at home, a devastating nor'west cyclone hit Broome, wiping out over twenty luggers and killing one hundred and forty crew. The 'blow' was early and unexpected; fleets had just put out to sea after lay-up. Like all his fellow pearlers, Dad lost men and boats (all were damaged, but some could be repaired). He was in trouble financially, having paid the crews for a full year's work, as was the custom. Mother wrote telling me about the willy-willy, explaining that while Fred and I would continue at school, my piano lessons must stop. This was good news as far as I was concerned – no more practising scales or being browbeaten by my well-meaning teacher. However, I also had to give up ballroom dancing classes, concerts in town and elocution lessons with the brilliant Miss Kavanagh, whom I idolised. Grandpa Sprang came to my parents' rescue, as he had always done, and Dad's carpenter,

Toshimoto, built a new lugger, *Gloria*, to add to the depleted fleet. The calamity didn't impact fully on my self-centred teenage mind and I got on with life as I knew it.

The school dance was a huge event every year, but could only be attended if you were fifteen or older. A formal invitation would be sent to a boy, and other preparations were made weeks in advance. In 1936 I became a senior, but like many of my friends, I was not yet fifteen. We were allowed to lean out of the bathroom windows on each side of the quad and look through the high set of windows running along the length of the hall to hear the band and catch glimpses of the girls in their long pretty dresses, their partners in black tie and dinner jackets. At the supper break they'd stroll over to the dining room for a buffet supper and we'd be able to see them properly under the lights streaming out into the dark. 'There's Percy Oliver,' someone would say – he was blond, handsome and Western Australia's gold-medal-winning champion swimmer, every girl's dream. I feverishly looked forward to being fifteen in April 1937.

It was finally my turn to attend the school dance. We talked about nothing else between lessons: who we were taking, what we were wearing. The day-girls knew lots of boys, and some boarders knew boys from ballroom dancing class, which made it easier for them. My quandary was not knowing any Perth boys at all. I didn't want to ask my brother, who at nineteen would have hated being my partner as much as I would have hated having him. Two mature and flirtatious friends of mine, quite at ease with the opposite sex, knew many Hale and Guildford students and said, 'Leave it to us.' They invited two Guildford boys as their partners, and between the four of them selected a boy for me. We sent formal invitations to our partners-to-be and duly received their acceptance replies.

The longed-for day finally arrived. I wore a rather shapeless pink dress with a full ankle-length skirt and silver sandals with small heels. Once I saw what everyone else was wearing – their dresses all seemed so much more fashionable than mine – I hated that dress! Nevertheless, I felt ready for my blind date. Our three Guildford Grammar partners arrived, smartly attired in black tie and dinner jacket, and I realised with a sinking heart the prank my friends had played on me. My two friends' boys were handsome and dashing sixteen-year-olds, one of whom was rumoured to have kissed a housemaid at Guildford. My partner towered over me – I later discovered he was the tallest boy in the school – while I was the shortest teenager at St Hilda's. We were both mortified, but danced the obligatory first dance together, my head coming up only as far as the middle button of his dinner jacket, as well as the supper dance and the last dance. Between dances the boys withdrew and the girls sat on chairs lining the hall. No-one mingled until the orchestra started up again. I was resigned to being a wallflower, but in the end several shorter boys asked me to dance, making my night.

During supper partners mixed again, though my partner and I barely spoke. We didn't know what to talk about, and were too embarrassed anyway. My two friends and their Guildford boys, boldly showing off, slipped into the cloak room, quickly embraced and snatched loud kisses as we passed, which caused scandalised giggles and much gossip for weeks afterwards.

Fred and I wrote frequently to each other, and in one letter he mentioned a boy called Edmund Haines. They'd become great chums, and Fred had discovered that Ed's sister, Mollie, was also a boarder at St Hilda's, though a year older than me. She seemed to me very grown up, warm and kind, and I admired her. Ed and Mollie came from the country; their parents owned a wheat and sheep property at Dangin, a few hours drive from Perth. Whenever they came to Perth to stay for a few days they'd take Ed, Mollie and Fred for outings, and on learning that I was at school with their daughter, they asked me to go along too.

I felt like one of the family immediately. Aunty Jean (Mrs Haines) exuded affectionate interest, and her husband, Uncle Guy, was an Englishman with a dry sense of humour. One year, the Haines family invited Fred and me to spend the winter holidays with them at Aunty Jean's mother's property, Lakemeres, also near Dangin. I looked forward to the visit, not just to spend time with the Haineses, but because it would be a new experience.

The end of term arrived, and we were picked up for the drive to Dangin. Mollie had invited Mura Carpenter, a boarder in her year, as well. The seven of us somehow fitted into the roomy car, though being the smallest, I had to sit on someone's knee. We finally drew up some time after dark to the sound of happy shouts of welcome. Aunty Jean's mother, Gran Woolley, and brother, sister-in-law and six nieces and nephews crowded around the car. Mollie and Edmund's Uncle Knox had built his home directly opposite his mother's, so the two long, low, rambling houses faced each other, forming a family compound, with weeping branches of peppertrees shading the short stretch between them. We newcomers were introduced and enthusiastically greeted, and I felt at home straightaway. We trooped into Gran Woolley's homestead and sat down to supper at an enormous table groaning with food.

Breakfast the following morning was no less impressive: there was porridge, milk straight from the cow, cream in several different stages of thickness, boiled and scrambled new-laid eggs, bacon, toast, farm butter. Meals at Dangin are a vivid memory, to say the least. The property, though mainly producing wheat and sheep, had an enormous vegetable garden, and there were chickens, cows and horses.

After breakfast Mollie's cousin Joan suggested we visit the stables. I was uneasy near horses, which seemed to me to be nervy and unpredictable beasts that would whinny and rear up for no reason, so I stood back. Joan proposed we go on a riding picnic the following day, which was eagerly seconded by everyone except me. All the cousins were accomplished riders – they seemed to practically live on their horses. 'I can't ride,' I muttered, but Joan briskly told me she'd put me on a quiet old gelding who was guaranteed not to streak off, buck, rear or throw me. His only fault, she informed me, was a tendency to stumble. I was not looking forward to it. We then explored the home paddocks, entirely different from Uncle Tom's farm at Langton Green in England: they were huge and yellow, rather barren-looking when not golden with wheat, and there were no dividing hedges or old stone walls.

We assembled the following morning under the peppertrees and I was helped onto a big cream-coloured nag for our excursion. We set off, Joan leading the way through the trees surrounding a lake. I managed to keep up and my steed behaved in spite of his frequent stumbles – I was nearly pitched straight over his head on one scary occasion. Eventually we dismounted and tethered our animals, and it was then that I came to grief. I neglected to tie up my horse properly, and while no-one was watching he ambled over to our picnic blanket and gobbled our sandwiches. I was mortified, but everyone laughed and assured me he'd done it many times before.

Soon afterwards, Ed said one morning at breakfast, 'What about driving to Weybridge to see how the house is getting on?' Weybridge was Ed, Mollie and their little brother Bernard's home, which was being renovated. We chorused 'Yes!' and Ed got out the car. He drove along the dry dusty road, which was at times as bumpy as driving over corrugated iron, even worse than the roads around Broome, until we turned into a driveway and stopped at a large square bungalow. The builders were laying floorboards, so we trod gingerly through a new room with a huge picture window. After a bit of exploration, Ed said to Fred, 'You can drive home if you like.' There was a mettlesome attraction between Mollie and my brother, so no-one was surprised when she scoffed, 'Fred, bet you can't drive.' I could see Fred was nettled. He flushed red and climbed into the driver's seat, Ed beside him. We girls sat in the back. Fred started the car, negotiated the drive and turned on to the road, where he crunched the gears as he tried to change them. Mollie taunted over his shoulder, 'You don't know how to drive!' Fred went redder and the car bumped faster over the corrugations. I began to feel frightened; Fred wasn't an experienced driver. The top-heavy car swerved to the right, then left, right again, and then hurtled upside down onto its roof. As it was going over I yelled, 'We're dead! We're all dead!' There was a final thud, then Mura remarked dryly, 'You're not, anyway!' A few minutes later we climbed through the open windows and shakily stood up, uninjured. We must have been due back at Lakemeres, because

Uncle Guy soon arrived in another car to find us. I was upset that my brother had caused the accident and smashed the car – he was distraught too – but Aunty Jean and Uncle Guy were wonderful and didn't blame anyone. I loved Mollie, but I knew that her taunting had badly undermined Fred's self-esteem on this occasion.

Our vacation was drawing to an end, but we were still having a marvellous time. At night after dinner we played cards, dressed up for charades, or went to country hops held in weatherboard Country Women's Association halls. We teenagers would gather inside while mothers congregated in the kitchen to prepare supper. Girls sat on upright chairs lining the walls, and the boys drew together in a male enclave at one end of the room. When a pianist began playing the latest hit tunes and traditional country dance music, boys proceeded towards us hopefuls, and eyed us up and down like buyers selecting heifers from the auction yards. I was very self-conscious, aware of my puppy fat, freckles and my nose, which would go red in spite of layers of powder. At one memorable dance, a dark-haired boy stopped unexpectedly in front of me, had a good look, then asked me to dance the Sir Roger de Coverley. I stood up and pranced vigorously with him around the crowded room. We all stopped for supper – sandwiches, cakes and fruit cups – then everyone went outside for fresh air. My dance partner, whose name was David, put his arm around my shoulders and walked me to a shadowy corner, where he planted an experimental kiss on my lips. It felt rather nice. But we didn't linger when the music started again – I went back to my seat and he wandered off to select another girl.

Just before going back to school, Mollie asked Gran Woolley if she would read our palms. Gran Woolley was reputed to have psychic gifts as a consequence of her Celtic ancestry, and we were all keen to know what lay ahead for us in our young lives. She must have used her discretion, foretelling nothing unpleasant. I went first, and Gran Woolley looked intently at my palm. After telling me a few simple things, she exclaimed that I was going to marry young and live a long distance away from Western Australia. Those were the days when few Western Australians moved from our lonely state across the Nullarbor to the east, let alone overseas. I thought it very exciting. Mollie was next, and Gran said with surprise that her granddaughter would live even further away than I would. Edmund, Bernard and Fred's futures all lay overseas too, she said.

Strangely, all these predictions would come true. I wonder now whether Gran Woolley sensed that World War II was approaching and would fling our generation far and wide – we certainly didn't, and thought only of carefree travel to exotic faraway places, not the cruel dispersion of Australia's young that war would soon bring.

One cold and misty morning we put our uniforms on ready for the long drive back to Perth and school. I still have a photograph taken by Edmund before our journey. We are lined up according to height, Fred first in a white shirt, tie and buttoned-up overcoat. Mollie is next to him, her long hair in plaits. Mura is next, her short dark hair framing her face, and then at the end there is me: a head shorter than everyone else. I felt a great sadness at leaving Aunty Jean and Uncle Guy, though Fred and I returned to Dangin a few times on open invitation before circumstances divided us all.

The year 1938 marked my last year at St Hilda's, but some of my friends had already moved on. Peggy Usher was attending Underwood's Business College so she'd be able to apply for an office job in Singapore. Nearly every girl who wasn't going to university went to Underwood's. Peggy kindly took me out for free weekends and days off. One of our outings was to see the sentimental film *Maytime*, with singing stars Nelson Eddy and Jeanette Macdonald. We ate Fantales and cried throughout the screening. Afterwards we agreed that *Maytime* was beautiful and *so* sad, and said in unison, 'Let's go to the afternoon show!' We bought more tickets and Fantales and cried again as we unwrapped and chewed our sweets, loving every minute.

My second and final school dance approached. Mother's Perth friends recommended a dressmaker in Hay Street, and the frock she made me was charming: an ivory taffeta splashed with small bouquets of flowers, cut on the cross to the ankles. There

*From left: Me, Mura, Mollie and Fred ready for
the long drive back to school after our holidays.*

was also a long-sleeved short jacket of an ivory, lightly beaded
quilted fabric to go with it. The dress was slimming and made
me look taller, especially with my silver high-heeled sandals.

I had met my school friend Judy Brisbane's cousin John,
who lived nearby at Peppermint Grove, at a weekend party. I
sent him a formal invitation, and he accepted. Judy and I were
pleased.

In the week before the dance, Dad arrived in Perth to see a
specialist for an ailment of his. Fred and I were there to meet
him at the wharf and escort him to the new Criterion Hotel in
the middle of town. We were to spend the weekend with Dad,
from Friday evening to Sunday, enjoying the luxury of hotel
life and rooms to ourselves.

Dad looked a new person as he walked off the ship. He was wearing a well-cut fawn suit with a waistcoat, and his face was pink, not its usual red. He didn't find fault with either of us. I decided during this visit that he was quite different away from Mother, though I had no idea why. Although he loved her obsessively, sparks flew when they were together. I realise now that these two people, one fiery and possessive, the other sparkling, charming but strongly independent, had both given up ingrained lifestyles to marry, expecting more from the other than either was able to give under the stressful emotional circumstances of their marriage.

On the Saturday morning of the dance, I was sitting alone in my hotel room, suffering teenage blues. Like all young people at one time or another, I was thinking about how frightened I was of dying. Dad knocked on the door to ask if I would like some morning tea. He could see I was miserable, so he came in and sat on the easy chair. Drawing me into his lap he said, 'Now, tell me what's the matter.' He didn't laugh off my fear, but spoke kindly to me for a long time until I felt better. I really loved Dad then, and knew he was a kind and understanding man underneath the bluff.

I set about preparing for the dance. Dad was coming too, as was Fred, as Mollie Haines's partner. I asked Dad if he'd give me some money to have my hair done and he readily agreed, pressing a new pound note into my hand. I hurried to a popular hairdresser in a nearby arcade and asked them to give my long tresses (still worn in plaits) a henna rinse. Young girls did not colour their hair in those days, but I longed for mine to be red instead of wishy-washy auburn. I was thrilled with the result, my father too, and none of my contemporaries ever forgot it – they talked for years afterwards about how Rosemary Goldie *dyed* her hair *red* for the school dance!

That evening there were lively foxtrots and traditional ballroom dances where the boys gently put one arm around their girl's waist, held her other hand and rhythmically proceeded around the dance floor. I enjoyed myself immensely and John was attentive and charming, but I couldn't bear to look at Dad dancing with Miss Small. He looked smooth and well-dressed in his white tie and tails, and was obviously enjoying himself, but he was dancing in such a funny, old-fashioned way, pumping my headmistress's arm up and down, like he did with Mother when they put a record on. It was the way couples had danced during World War I and in the 1920s – all the older generation pranced around like that, but not us!

Nonetheless, the dance that year was a great success, nothing like the disaster of the year before. I was amazed how self-assured I had become in only twelve months.

The happiest memories of my five years at St Hilda's are of that final year in 1938. All the girls in my class were preparing for the Junior Certificate. Some were brainy at fifteen, others average at sixteen, like me. I knew I'd be leaving school in December and going back to Broome, but I wanted to return to Perth the following year and learn commercial art. I was well aware I'd have to talk Dad around to this idea. I studied my chosen subjects diligently for the Junior – English, history, French and domestic science were my favourites – cramming like all the others as the exams approached.

Butterflies in my tummy, I sat the tests, and felt quietly confident that I had done enough to pass well, but I would not know the results till after Christmas. Then December came, and I said a blithe farewell to St Hilda's and my schooldays, and a temporary farewell to my very dear pals, and went back to Broome.

It was a relief to be home and not have to study anymore, and at first I basked in the relaxing atmosphere. But those halcyon days didn't last. Once the holidays were over most of my contemporaries left Broome. They were continuing at various schools for the Leaving Certificate, starting or going back to university like Fred, or training in other fields. Some were planning to leave Broome when they were able to. My only friends who remained were Heather Reynolds, Flora Milner (Sheila was away at teachers' college) and Margery Stanton. Pam was in Broome occasionally, but she and Greg spent many weeks in Darwin where they had further pearling interests, and often travelled. They holidayed in Singapore and Australia's eastern cities. I looked forward to the time they spent in Broome as Pam lifted everyone's spirits wherever she was. Pat McDaniel, tall and gorgeous, was also still in Broome. A few years older than me, she spent half her time with the married set and half with us younger singles. Even Daisy, who was twelve and would soon be starting at St Hilda's, was leaving Broome, further reducing my social circle.

There were married couples of different age groups living in the pearling town, a few unmarried 'bank boys' and other businessmen not interested in courting naïve young girls with strict parents, and several local youths who paired off with girls prepared to stay in Broome. There were no distractions for young people; there were just too few of us. I wanted badly to go back to Perth and do a course in commercial art.

Mother knew I wanted to study art – I'd been considered a talented artist at St Hilda's – but she said I'd have to speak to Dad. I waited for what seemed like the right moment and, heart in mouth, approached him. The reply was a resounding no. There was no money in it, I must be able to support myself, I should learn something sensible that would not be wasted, he said. If I learnt anything, he added, it would have to be shorthand and typing, and for that I could go to the convent and learn from one of the nuns.

I was fed up with Broome; it was infuriatingly isolated, and I was dreadfully bored. I settled on learning typing – I thought it might just help me get away to Perth somehow. My teacher was Sister Cecilia, a sweet young woman shrouded in a white veil and neck-to-ankle habit. I asked her repeatedly, wasn't she hot? She always replied no, and somehow made me believe it. We sat on a side verandah of the convent while she instructed me and we chatted together about everything.

For my seventeenth birthday, Dad gave me the latest model typewriter. I practised on it at home, typing business letters for him and articles he'd written to send to the Perth newspapers about interesting events in Broome. Judging from his many scribblings – most of which were published – he was a frustrated journalist! I remember typing one letter from Dad to the federal government on behalf of the Pearlers' Association: sampans from Japan were illegally gathering shell in Australian territorial waters during lay-up and shell beds were being depleted. Our pearlers were finding it hard to bring home enough for themselves when they put out to sea after lay-up; the boom time of pearling had passed as cheaper synthetics were being used in many industries. Dad suggested the government send a battleship once a year around the north-west to patrol our waters. Today a similar idea is being discussed, but this time illegal immigrants are the target.

Margery, Flora, Heather and I laughed and relaxed together, danced without partners and tried to tap-dance to the latest jazz and swing music on our gramophones. They, too, were waiting to go back to Perth. Fred came to visit from university, and together we celebrated his twenty-first birthday on 8 July 1939. Mother bought masses of shelled oysters from the Japanese oyster-man at the back door, and used her magic touch to blend flavours and make generous 'cocktails', to eat with a spoon from individual glasses as a special entrée for the festive meal.

Later, Fred and I were sitting and talking together on the front steps, brushed by the sweeping pandanus leaves. I told him how miserable I was, how trapped I felt, as though I'd be living in Broome, this sparsely settled 'island' in the middle of the Indian Ocean, forever. He was sympathetic, and assured me I'd leave some day.

Walking home one afternoon from my lesson at the convent, I called in at the Gregorys' house to see Pam, which I often did when she was in Broome. She looked cool and pretty in a pink linen sundress. I had on a David Jones mail-order blue and green dirndl. There were still no decent clothing shops in Broome – everything had to be purchased from far away or material bought from Broome's Chinese drapers and clothes made up by the dressmaker. As for window shopping, that was unheard of. We settled into the cane easychairs on the verandah and Pam brought me an ice-cold soda water. She may have had something stronger, but with my naïve schoolgirl outlook and very strict father, I'd never tasted alcohol. We were talking and laughing when there was a knock on the door, and to my amazement two handsome young airmen walked in and were welcomed by Pam. She served them beers and we chatted happily together. One of the airmen, an attractive captain, said something complimentary to me. I laughed delightedly and thought no more about it. Later, at home, the telephone rang and it was the captain, asking me to go with him to the Sun Pictures that night. Of course I accepted on the spot, but when I told Dad he went bright red and blew up: 'My daughter is not going anywhere with any man until he asks my permission!' Red myself with indignation, I replied, 'But Dad, what do I do? I said yes.' 'He'll have to ask me before you go anywhere with him, my girl,' was the response. I've forgotten the sequence of events, but the airman did ring for my father's permission to take me out, and didn't call the whole thing off. But I can guess his feelings!

At seven-thirty I heard one of the two Broome taxis come down the road and stop at our front gate. There were footsteps on the shell path, up the steps, the rustle of pandanus leaves beside the open front door, and then the airman was standing there. He was good-looking in a rugged, masculine way, with broad shoulders, light brown hair and twinkling blue eyes. He was wearing the RAAF tropical uniform of khaki shorts and short-sleeved shirt, epaulettes on the shoulders, long khaki socks and polished shoes. Mother, Dad and I walked along the verandah to meet him. I'd brushed my long reddish hair into a roll around my face, put on Max Factor make-up to cover my freckles and wore a green silk dress nipped in at the waist and with a flared skirt. I had on my highest heels to make me look taller than my five feet. To my immense relief, Dad was welcoming, even charming. Of course I never had any qualms about introducing anyone to Mother. Formalities over, my beau and I walked to the taxi and were driven to the cinema.

The film had started when we arrived, and the airman led me down to the deckchairs in the front section in the dark. During the first reel change he told me about the various star formations we could see – the saucepan, Southern Cross, Milky Way – all clearly defined in the immense inky Broome sky. At interval we went over the road to Ellie's cafe and sipped their famous icy lemon squash. The airman told me he was from Melbourne, that he was twenty-five and had recently lost his mother. I was seventeen – eight years younger! We went back through the cigarette-smoking crowd that was spilling out of the Roebuck Bay pub, to see the rest of the movie.

During the next reel change I learnt about clouds: cumulus, cirrus, cumulonimbus. As the film was finishing, before the lights had come on, the captain led me outside and into a waiting taxi. I did not realise that the story was already going around town: 'Buddy Goldie is going out with an air force officer!' We arrived back at my house, he escorted me to the door, and after I'd thanked him we said a chaste goodnight. There had been no touching, no attempts to kiss me, not even handholding, though in my childlike innocence I had not expected any.

I had no idea then of male urges; even if I had, it would have been out of the question with me. I had been brought up, as had most women of my generation, with the message that becoming pregnant before marriage was shameful. Abortions were dangerous and easy contraception was unknown. Not to mention that if the airman had seduced me I'm sure Dad would have been after him with a shotgun. Nevertheless, the next morning I heard an aeroplane roaring overhead, ran outside, and there he was, buzzing over the house and waving. I waved back, thrilled to bits.

I learnt a lesson of reality from my encounter with the airman. When World War II began in Europe that year, the RAAF set up a base in Darwin, knowing that the Japanese could strike Australia at any time. They sent down a coast-watching plane with two pilots to Broome once a week. Dad was made the Military Intelligence Officer for the north-west coast, and the pilots reported to him, so I met many of them and saw my original airman again several times. He came to drinks and dinner, and invited us to look over his plane, a Wirraway, at the airfield one evening. He was always kind to me and seemed to enjoy my company. Tora, a self-styled clairvoyant, used to say: 'Captain like Buddy, he soon engagee.' I thought so too, until one day I found out he and his fellow pilot were taking barmaids to Cable Beach at night – and not for a swim! I was furious – a skinny tough-looking peroxide-blonde barmaid! All Broome knew, but I decided not to cry; he wasn't going to have the honour of my tears! The airman dented my heart a little at the time, but the experience was invaluable and made me more mature. I heard later that he flit-

ted from woman to woman, a born Casanova, and not the kind
of man I would have been happy with at all.

In September 1939 it was announced that Britain was at war
with Germany and Italy, which meant that we in the British
dominions were at war too. Mother, Dad, Daisy and I were listening to the wireless, a new and handsome freestanding piece
with excellent reception, which we'd tuned in to Perth for the
news. Usually we listened to a Dutch-language station trans-
mitted from Java, even though we couldn't understand the
commentary we enjoyed the music. It was easier to receive
because it was closer to us in the north than the radio from
Perth. That evening I remember Mother crying and Dad's
sombre expression as the announcer said that war had come
again, twenty-one years after the end of World War I. I felt
anxious, but not particularly frightened; Japan had always been
a concern, but Europe felt like a world away. I had never paid
much attention to international affairs and, like most of my
friends, lived only for the moment.

Japan had not yet come into the conflict, but had a clearly

unsympathetic attitude towards the Allies. We felt the tension from some members of the large Japanese community in Broome – though up till this point there had been a mutual respect, even a liking, between us. A fine Japanese gentleman, who owned a respected general store in town, would occasionally come to our house for afternoon tea. He wore an immaculate white suit, his pretty Japanese wife in Western clothes. Before his arrival we always put his gift to us, a framed photograph of his family, in a prominent place.

In early 1940, Mother travelled to Perth with Daisy, who was then nearly thirteen years old, to settle her into boarding school at St Hilda's. Dad said it was high time I got a job and began to put away some savings; I agreed, thinking it the quickest way to Perth. He arranged a meeting with the postmaster, who interviewed me for a vacancy at the manual telephone exchange, and I was put on for several hours in the morning and again later in the afternoon. There was only one operator at a time on the antiquated switch. Three of us worked at staggered hours on weekdays, and someone else took over for nights and weekends.

Heather Reynolds was another of the weekday girls, and showed me how to put the plugs in and out of the machine's holes and listen with earphones to the subscriber's voice when their number shrilled. There was a microphone-like contraption to speak into while the caller requested the number he or she wanted, and we had to write in pencil in small squares on thin white cardboard the few digits belonging to the caller.

I went to and from work by bicycle, though if it was dark Dad picked me up or dropped me off in the car. I was terribly bored by it all, but glad to put my earnings into a savings account. Margery Stanton warned me not long after I started that the postmaster made passes at young girls; I noticed that he stared at me in a funny way but left me alone. Dad would have exploded and run the man out of Broome had he tried anything – he probably knew that. I think now, though, that he may have had some easy conquests in the past.

If I was off duty until the middle of the day, kind Phyllis McDaniel – Terry, Nolan and Pat's mother – who lived nearby, would invite me to her house for lunch, and I could lie down afterwards in the spare room for a siesta. She was quite bohemian for the day, preferring to work in her beautiful garden than to socialise and play bridge. She was very good to me, and I once heard her sigh and say, 'Poor Louis,' when we were discussing my years in England. Her sympathy for Dad, left at home alone for four years, was obvious. All our friends loved my father; it was interesting to hear her words, and I realised I had rarely wondered how Dad had coped while we were away. I knew he had gone to sea a lot.

Phyllis and I talked about art together. She had lived in Sydney's eastern suburbs as a girl and had studied with a well-known artist of the day. Sometimes when I was free we drove to faraway beaches, where we would set up our easels and paint. I learnt to appreciate the dreamy pastel colours of endless sparkling white sand, the subtle shades of blue in the ocean, the pink and milky opalescent tinges of sky.

Mother was away from Broome for four weeks. During that time, Dad and I got on well together; there were no clashes of will, and I recall those weeks as peaceful and friendly. We went out to dinner with friends, or they came to us. The first time we entertained, Tora set the table and arranged the cutlery. Eyeing it critically, I reset everything, placing it like Mother did, remembering the correct ways employed at New Farm. Tora saw this as he peered from the kitchen and, clicking his teeth as he angrily pattered over to the table, he moved everything back as it had been before. I thought as hostess (and as a cocksure seventeen-year-old who had not learnt to be diplomatic) that it should be done my way, so I rearranged it again. Tora flew out of the kitchen, losing his temper entirely this time, and screamed out insults before promptly leaving for Japtown, where he stayed until Mother returned. Ede and Morrie Lyons came for dinner, which was luckily already cooked. A fill-in maid looked after things following this episode until Mother came home, but I have regretted my behaviour ever since.

Mother returned from Perth, having left Daisy at St Hilda's, and life went back to its usual routine. I began my campaign to leave Broome in earnest. Things had flared up between my parents once more and Dad and I couldn't get on either – my persistence annoyed him. He was unable to comprehend a teenager's dislike of Broome with its limited society, because he thought it paradise on earth. Mother knew I needed to go to the city where I could pursue my own interests. She had always received an allowance from Grandpa Sprang, and she said she'd help financially. The pearling industry was in serious straits; the war just about putting an end to the trade as we had known it. Dad would have found it difficult to help even if he'd wanted to. I also had my 'running away' money, saved from my job at the post office.

Mother raised the issue on my behalf with Dad, who finally agreed to my departure – as I had become a thorn in his side with my nagging, he may have been relieved. When Bishop Frewer was back in Broome after visiting the outposts of his huge diocese his advice was sought. 'Where should Rosemary stay in Perth, m'lord?' Perth, or any city, was to Dad a big bad place where girls went astray. 'Mrs Sarell's boarding house,' said the bishop without hesitation.

Mrs Sarell was a widow, an impoverished gentlewoman who had turned her two-storey house in Ord Street, West Perth, into a haven for students and young people whose homes were a long way from the universities and other learning institutions. Fred had stayed there on occasion when he wasn't living in his rooms at St George's College at Perth University. Sarell's was shabby, as places were in those days, but clean, and young people from well-known families stayed there. Letters were sent and a room booked for me. I was over the moon with joy and anticipation.

One evening as Dad and I were talking about my imminent departure, he said, 'Has your mother spoken to you about certain things?' 'What things?' I replied, nonplussed. Dad wasted no further time being delicate. 'I don't want you bringing a kid back here for us to look after!' he grumped. I was outraged. Didn't he realise I had a healthy respect for my body?

Mother and I had never talked about sex, a topic hardly ever discussed between parents and children in that era. However, I can now understand Dad's concern about my leaving. And a worldwide fear at the time was the white slave trade, which females of all ages talked about in hushed voices. The belief was that you could be sitting alone in a public place – a cinema, a hotel lobby, a train station – and a respectable-looking stranger next to you might prick your arm with a hypodermic needle, drug you and spirit you away to be sold to an Asian brothel. The method of kidnapping may have been embellished when I heard it, but it was an accepted danger at the time. A send-up even appeared in the film *Thoroughly Modern Millie*: two pig-tailed Chinese men shuffled along in slippers at midnight, holding a covered 'laundry basket', inside which was a girl to be sold into the slave trade!

The night before I was to catch the state ship to Perth, there was a farewell party for me. People who'd known me all my life, as well as the handful of friends my age left in Broome, wrote messages in my autograph album. I felt a great impatience to leave, and to begin my adult life. Trunk packed, I could hardly wait until morning, to board the ship and shake the red dust off my feet. It was a dream come true.

Finally, the moment arrived. Mother and Dad saw me off. The jetty was crowded with other passengers and their well-wishers, businessmen, and women going to Perth to see family or to holiday. I was sharing a cabin with a middle-aged lady my parents knew. I was happy to sleep in the top bunk and watch the sea from our porthole, daydreaming about living at Sarell's, studying at Underwood's Business College with other girls, seeing school pals and going to parties. This time as we hugged goodbye I didn't mind leaving Mother. My escape was all I could think about, my excitement at a fever pitch. At last we pulled away from the jetty and I waved until my parents were just specks in the distance. Then I went to my cabin, stared intently out of the porthole at the high scarlet cliffs of Broome as we slipped past them, and firmly declared: 'Goodbye red cliffs, I'm never coming back!'

Epilogue

War finally came to Broome. The people of Western Australia had for years been apprehensive that the Japanese would invade; more so than their countrymen in the eastern states who, perhaps because they were separated from the west by endless barren desert plains, did not feel the danger so acutely. However, the invasion of China in the 1930s, the devastating fall of Singapore, the occupation of nearby islands and the push towards Java represented a real and encroaching threat. The bombing of Pearl Harbor on 7 December 1941 could not be mistaken for anything other than an act of aggression towards the Allies. People feared that Australia would be next. The country was on alert.

After the fall of Singapore in early 1942, it was decided that the European women and children in Broome would be evacuated by ship to Perth. Daisy was at St Hilda's, Fred at university and I was newly married and living in Sydney. Mother, after twenty-five years in the far-flung outpost she had come to call home, was not unhappy to leave. Family money had melted away in vain attempts to bolster our ailing fleet. Greg had been right – the future lay in cultured pearls. The old guard would not believe it; those who did, such as Nick Paspaley, who worked hard after the war to build up Paspaley Pearls, made a fortune.

It is fair to say that Mother had come to terms with her life in Broome, though she never got used to the armies of nocturnal cockroaches thick on the kitchen floor, the mosquitoes, sandflies and hornets that blew into the house night and day, the deadly scorpions, centipedes and snakes. She was a much-loved member of the Broome community, producing concerts and plays, sharing her warm, outgoing nature and sunny charm. She remained a loyal and faithful wife to her war-ravaged husband. Many years later, my younger son, Ian, visited Broome and met old Jimmy Chi, son of the Jimmy I knew. He told Ian he remembered my mother fondly. There is no doubt the life she led was a far cry from the one she might have had in England, but the arid outback and red Kimberley obviously needed her more.

Once in Perth, though, Mother began to live again. There were outlets for her artistic talents, and she took part in repertory theatre and acted in radio plays. Her health improved and she was happy. One far-sighted friend suggested that with her RADA training she should sit for a speech and drama teacher's exam, which she did, passing with flying colours. It led to a fulfilling future when she moved to Sydney after my father's death.

Initially Dad remained in Broome. He didn't listen to Mother's pleas and arguments to leave when war broke out. He and his pearling companions were going to stay on and fight the Japs every inch of the way if the buggers came, he assured her. I was told many years later of his exploits and courage when the Japanese forces did indeed arrive. He was a brave, stubborn man.

I have a copy of Dad's typewritten account for army head-quarters of what happened in Broome when the Japanese bombed the town on 3 March 1942, shortly after the Darwin bombings. This was war at its stealthiest and ugliest. Men, women and children, most of them Dutch evacuees from Java, were in flying boats in Roebuck Bay en route to Perth, about to take off. They had spent the night on board while the aircraft refuelled, due to the difficulties disembarking on Broome's ten-metre tides and the lack of accommodation in the town. At about 9.30 am, Japanese planes flew over Broome and began strafing the refugee craft, and within minutes all fifteen were either sinking or ablaze. The casualties were horrific; some forty evacuees perished in the flying boats, or were taken by sharks as they tried to swim to shore.

By 10.30 am, the Japanese aircraft turned north to return to their base at Koepang. All Allied aircraft at Broome had been destroyed, as had the airfield. Today, if you walk quickly as far as you can when the tide is out in Roebuck Bay, you'll see the wreckage of the Dutch flying boats before the tide rushes back in. The bodies of the refugees were taken ashore and reverently buried.

After the attack, Dad's life and livelihood were in tatters. The old seadog put on a brave front. The damaged luggers were burnt in line with Australia's scorched-earth policy, to prevent any successful invaders from salvaging them. The rest were confiscated by the government and were to be sailed in convoy to Fremantle. My father was put in charge of this expedition. Our house and business were abandoned. Once in Perth, Dad made the best of his new life, joined the army and became an officer. Because his expertise lay in intelligence and in maritime activity around the Western Australian coast, he was not put on active service but based in Geraldton.

Mother joined him there and enjoyed the civilised surroundings. Geraldton was a small city, but had all amenities –

including flushing lavatories. Eventually, when the war ended, my parents bought a pleasant bungalow in Cottesloe and found peace with each other. Dad led legal proceedings against the government to reimburse pearlers for the loss of their luggers, the outcome of which was in the pearlers' favour. He was offered the job of Harbour Master at Fremantle, and was glad to accept, so his life could once again be dedicated to the sea. There were other master pearlers in Perth, who would gather with Dad over whiskeys and soda to retell old yarns, dream old dreams and find consolation in each other's company.

Dad died of a sudden heart attack in 1950.

Rosef, the lugger my father named for Fred and me, is still in existence, now owned by a boat devotee in Perth, who restored her, renamed her *Rose-F*, and sails her for pleasure.

My mother moved to Sydney and made a new life for herself giving speech training in schools and judging at eisteddfods all over the country. She used to say to me, 'When I was in Broome looking at the deserted landscape, I'd pray, "Please God, give me back the years the locusts have eaten."' And God did. Her new life lasted exactly twenty-five years, the total number of years she had spent in Broome.

Though he didn't win the Rhodes scholarship, my brother Fred enjoyed a long and illustrious career. Having graduated from university, he joined the First Australian Parachute Battalion during World War II. Mother bought a house in Castlecrag, Sydney, and made a home for Fred there after the war while he furthered his studies. He then embarked on a career that would see him become a much-respected scholar in international law. He had graduated from the University of Western Australia before the war with first class honours in law, and later earned both a bachelor's and master's degree from the University of Sydney, two diplomas from the Hague Academy of International Law, and spent a year at Harvard Law School. He married an Englishwoman, Sheila, and held a number of academic appointments throughout the world, eventually becoming an American citizen and settling at Syracuse University College in 1969. He retired in 1989 and was named professor emeritus of law at that university. Though retired, Fred continued working until his sudden death from a heart attack at the age of seventy-two.

Like Fred, Daisy loved the academic life. She did well at St Hilda's and continued to the University of Western Australia, where she acquired a BSc with honours. She married the professor of organic chemistry from the university, Phillip Jefferies, and had two daughters and a son. When her children left home, Daisy returned to university to study accounting, but was forced to abandon the course when she was diagnosed with cancer. In remission, she began teaching science part-time at Hollywood High School in Perth. Later, she developed a range of skincare products under the brand name Daisy, but sadly this venture was cut short when the cancer returned. Daisy died tragically young at the age of fifty-two.

Tora, like the vast majority of the Japanese community in Australia, was interned when war broke out with Japan. I often asked my parents after the war if they knew what had happened to him, but they had not been able to trace him and thought he may have died in the camp. I remember asking him once, in the period leading up to the war, 'Tora, Japan want come here?' He said vehemently, 'No, no, Russia! Russia!' and imitated a soldier's march holding an imaginary rifle. He thought Japan would be far too busy holding Russia at bay to bother about distant Australia.

Jerry and Topsy also disappeared. It was thought they may have gone bush when the Japanese attacked Broome.

My cousin Kitty married a BBC foreign correspondent, Dick Williams, and together they lived a glamorous life in many parts of the world. Their travels and Dick's work allowed them to meet many interesting and prominent people, and they were close friends with authors Ian Fleming, Lawrence Durrell and others. Kitty and I stayed in touch and visited each other when we could. In later years, after the sudden death of her husband, Kitty bought a cottage in Lincolnshire, near the lovely old farm at Barley Cliff that Aunt Joy and Uncle Fred had moved to, and remained there until her death in 2000. She was in her early eighties.

My Aunt Gay, in spite of the jealousy and resentment she had harboured towards my mother in earlier times, came to visit my parents in Perth and stayed nearly a year. She and Mother got on better than they ever had, and found a measure of peace in their relationship.

Pam Gregory left Broome just before the Japanese attack, though, characteristically, she had been determined to stay on, and had only gone at her father's insistence. She was on the last boat to leave, and was safely at Geraldton three days later when the attack occurred. Greg was in Darwin, as Pam had been before he sent her to Broome for her safety. By 1935 he had moved half his fleet there and opened a new office. He had also purchased a million and a half acres of property near Katherine in the Northern Territory. Greg immediately offered his help after the bombing in Darwin, and worked piloting American ships out of Darwin Harbour. Several months later he moved to Perth to an apartment overlooking the river, where Pam joined him and was again his constant companion. He died of a stroke on 22 December 1942. Pam married Commander William Charles Nielsen of the US Navy, who was stationed in Fremantle, and after the war she moved to the States, following her husband through thirteen different duty stations. She now lives in Los Altos, California.

My friends from school and the school ships saw an end to their carefree lives when the Japanese entered World War II. Many had to flee their homes and abandon everything they had. Many of the boys and young men were imprisoned in POW camps such as Changi, and most, including Gerald Usher, my friend Peggy's brother, did not survive. Peggy and her mother escaped Singapore by boat, not knowing its destination, and eventually reached South Africa. Peggy had left behind her husband, an RAF pilot, who was later killed on D-day. Peggy later remarried and had four children.

As foretold by Gran Woolley, Mollie Haines married an American serviceman and settled in San Francisco, and Ed joined the air force and was stationed in Britain, where he married an English girl. Their younger brother, Bernard, was also in the air force. He was shot down over Germany in the war and taken prisoner. He survived but remained single, travelling and living all over the world.

After the war, Margot Field worked for the Australian Department of Foreign Affairs in several countries, including Ceylon (now Sri Lanka), Ghana, USSR, South Korea and the United States, where, in San Francisco, she met her future husband, Rear Admiral Edward Carmick. He and Margot had a very happy marriage, and after his death she moved back to Perth where she still lives. She and Pam met again in San Francisco and resumed their childhood friendship. Sadly, we gradually lost touch with our other childhood friends.

My teenage beau, Gordon Reynolds, became a successful Sydney businessman whose hobby was sailing. Gordon's passion for the sea began in Broome, and later in life he belonged to several distinguished yacht clubs, including the Middle Harbour Yacht Club and the Cruising Yacht Club of Australia. He skippered many yachts in the Sydney to Hobart race. His crowning achievement was managing the Australian team for the Admiral's Cup for several years, held at Cowes in England. His team won in 1967. Gordon married his pretty wife, Sylvia, in 1942.

I was delighted in later life to meet my cousins on my father's side, Allan and Geoff, Dad's beloved sister Daisy's boys. We'd had no contact with them in childhood because of my father's disinheritance from his family, but they all became very special to me when we met in Sydney. Allan, a globetrotter with film-star good looks, had lived in London since he was twenty-one, where he became prominent as a producer and director of many well-known hit plays. He knew all the stars of the day and mixed in London's high society. He remained a bachelor.

Geoff's many talents lay in different directions from Allan's. No two brothers could have been more different. Geoff was dark and good-looking, with a great sense of humour and wit. He loved playing practical jokes. My cousin worked hard for causes he believed in, and he and his wonderful wife Elizabeth were great fundraisers for charity. Allan and Geoff have both died, but Elizabeth and their children are part of my treasured family today.

When my ship arrived at the Fremantle wharves from Broome, I stepped into my longed-for new life. Fred met me and escorted me to Sarell's in West Perth. I had my own room, but shared a bathroom, complete with chip heater, with the other girls. The boys had rooms on the other side of the house. I unpacked and went down to dinner (we were served three wholesome meals a day), where I met all the other young people who were staying there, and marvelled at how sophisticated they seemed. I was the youngest.

Everyone was talking about an absent boarder, John Hemphill, who was in Sydney visiting his family but would be back soon, it seemed. He was obviously very popular. I met John when he returned, and though he was four years older than me, and we moved in different crowds, we became friends. He was living in Perth because his family firm, J. A. Hemphill & Sons, wheat and flour shippers, had a branch there. I admired him from afar, but one day he told me he'd fallen in love and wanted to marry me. He was the nicest young man I'd ever known: lean, dark, intense, kind, yet strongly masculine. In spite of my father's objections – he was concerned that I was not yet twenty-one, but in any case he tended to object to everything! – we decided to marry before John went to Sydney to join the 2/6th Armoured Regiment with his youngest brother, Geoffrey. I was nineteen, John twenty-three.

Mother came from Broome for the wedding, which was held on 7 November 1941 at St Mary's Church in West Perth, and the reception was at her club, the Karrakatta Club. Dad could not attend, because the two weeks' travelling time to Perth and back would have kept him away from the business for too long. When congratulatory telegrams were read out there was one that said: 'Here's hoping the two babes don't get lost in the wood!' And our friends' wishes for us came true: John and

I had sixty-one blissful years together until John's death in 2003 at the age of eighty-five.

A few days after our marriage, John and I sailed in the *Katoomba* for Sydney. Because it was wartime, the ship had to be blacked out after dark to evade any stealthy German shipping, but the trip was uneventful, and for us, extremely happy. We came into Sydney Harbour on a sunny November morning and were greeted with an unforgettable sight. I marvelled at the green and cream ferries busily crossing from one side of the harbour to the other, the beautiful houses built right to the water's edge in green bushland, the huge expanse of sparkling blue water. Sydney was a seductive city and I fell in love with it.

We were met by John's father and brother, and travelled along the lush North Shore to Killara, past scarlet flame trees, purple-blue jacarandas and masses of blue hydrangeas, quite unlike Perth's pink ones. I was greeted warmly at John's family home, and his large circle of friends drew me into their midst and made me feel immediately at ease.

John soon joined his brother Geoffrey in B Squadron of the 2/6th Armoured Regiment. The sad partings began, but with many of the other wives I followed the regiment, staying in hotels in country towns including Tamworth and Singleton. When John had leave we travelled back to Killara and spent time with his family there. The dreadful day came when John and Geoffrey had to sail for New Guinea, where they were to fight at Buna and Sananda. John was particularly ill during this period of service.

I had wanted a baby, a part of John in case he never came back, and it was our good fortune that I quickly fell pregnant. Our first son, Richard, always known as Dick, was born by caesarean section after a long trial labour at Sydney's Crown Street Hospital in 1943. I had complications and nearly died. Two weeks later John arrived home on leave. He was just seven stone and bright yellow from Atebrin tablets, which he'd been given to combat malaria, though he contracted it badly anyway; quinine was unavailable for troops. He told me he'd had two dreams one night in which he'd vividly seen me at death's door. I was not surprised at this as he was always extremely sensitive.

John's health deteriorated during his New Guinea campaign and he was discharged into civilian life. His mother had died only a few years earlier and his father, now gravely ill, died shortly after Dick was born. He was delighted, though, to be able to sit up and hold his first grandchild before he died.

After John's father's death, a relative attempted to snatch away John's and his siblings' inheritance in the family company. Though legal action was instigated by two kindly uncles who were prominent in the community and some compensation was received, John's hopes of entering the family company were dashed. Trying to make the best of a bad situation, I said to him, 'Let's do our own thing, we can use the money to get started. Much better than having regrets for the rest of your life.' So we did just that.

Our second son, Ian, was born in 1949. Shortly afterwards, we bought a large orange orchard at Dural with two houses on it, one an ugly brick residence, the other a pretty little weatherboard cottage. The property was in the Hills District, over an hour's drive from Sydney's centre. Within a year a huge blow fell on Hills orange-growers when orchards along the soldier settlements of the Murray River began producing bigger, unblemished oranges. Everyone with citrus orchards in the Hills District was affected. Though we tried other paths, we were finally forced to sell most of our land, keeping five acres, and moving from the big house into the workman's cottage.

We decided to set up a nursery, and the idea of selling herbs came to us. Nobody was selling a wide variety of herbs then, only the familiar parsley, sage, thyme, marjoram, chives and mint. A friend recently back from a trip to Europe had given us a dozen packets of seeds for herbs I knew of from my time there. John sowed them successfully and we hunted far and wide for other herbaceous plants. We had the old favourites, but we also had basil, oregano, savory, chervil, rocket, coriander, angelica and many more largely unknown in Australia at that time.

Though everything we had tried previously had fallen through, this time things were different. Eager customers flocked to us. We branched into herbal products, like fragrant potpourri made from recipes in one of my old books, and we built a double-walled herb garden, New Farm style. Somerset Cottage Herbs and Spices was born.

We were full of enthusiasm and loved what we were doing; John with his practical hands and good business sense, me with my memories of New Farm and love of history and romance.

News about us spread through the Sydney community and we were inundated with customers. We expanded and expanded, and the media swarmed in on us. We were asked to give talks to groups, trembling at first, taking Dr Bach's homoeopathic Rescue Remedy to make us brave. I began to write books about herbs, which have been reprinted many times over the years. John and I also wrote some books together, which was even more fulfilling.

Our boys grew up and were both successful in their own ways. Dick's academic mind led him to the University of Sydney, where he studied science and engineering, graduating with honours. He later completed a Masters in Business Management. He now has his own firm and works as a consulting engineer in Brisbane, where he lives with his wife Elizabeth, their children nearby.

Ian worked with us, taking exams in business management before studying drama. During his first year at the National Institute of Dramatic Art he met his wife, also Elizabeth, and together they now run their very successful venture, 'Herbies', as today's experts on the huge variety of spices now on offer. They make their own superb blends and are themselves a wonderful combination.

We had a blissful time at Dural for nearly forty years, our life in herbs a long, successful saga full of memories. I would like to turn back the clock and be there still, walking around our garden, picking, smelling, tasting and talking about our magical herbs with our customers.

People often asked me, and still do, 'How did you know

herbs would take off?' We answered that we didn't, but looking back, I wonder if there is 'a destiny that shapes our ends' and that perhaps we were guided in every direction by a guardian angel. I have always felt there is a folk memory built into human beings of herbs and their qualities; something that is a part of the earth from which we all came. Whatever the truth, I have been blessed.

In 1996 my family urged me to return to Broome and 'lay ghosts'.

John and I flew in from Sydney via Ayers Rock airport in the middle of August – the cool dry season, although it was still hot. When we emerged from our plane and walked across the blazing tarmac, the pretty airport, now an oasis of palm trees and bougainvillea, looked quite different from the arid airfield surrounded by scrub that had serviced the few light aircraft and air force planes in my day. I knew that Broome had been transformed by the discovery of unlimited spring water about twenty years before our visit, but this evidence of the change was startling.

We drove to the Cable Beach Club Resort on sealed roads

with roundabouts, although the same silver-grey bush and deep orange earth I remembered were on either side. The primitive tyre-track we had travelled on in Dad's car was long gone.

As I looked out, I discovered that I was delighted by the amazing colour contrasts I had once tried to avoid in my artwork; contrasts for which this tiny, unique place is now famous.

The resort was a complete shock. Lord Alistair McAlpine's vision for recreating Broome was magnificent, a combination of Asian and European styles, with colourful, low, corrugated-iron buildings set in landscaped gardens with small lakes and water plants, darting gauzy dragonflies, curving Asian bridges and luxurious swimming pools. It was all enchanting, and all made possible by the spring water. My mother and other pearlers' wives could have lived happily here now with the ever-present air-conditioning, flushing lavatories, running water, diverse range of shops and restaurants, and Perth only a few hours' away by plane.

Cable Beach was another story. The pristine, deserted, pearl-white sands of my childhood were now full of people and strings of camels for the tourists. There had been no camels anywhere in Broome when I lived there.

A friendly taxi driver took us to my old house and, since he knew the owners, introduced us to one of them, Libby, who generously invited us to look around.

Much had changed but it was still recognisable. I felt dazed. Where was my family? Instead of the activity and bustle I remembered, the house was silent and eerie. Libby said, 'The house is haunted, you know.'

Amazed, I answered, 'But it was only built by my parents in 1919!'

Libby told me that the house had a reputation for haunting, and that when she was alone she often felt a benign presence. It dawned on me that this was Dad, who had adored Broome and the house. His soul was unsettled, perhaps by the struggle between his Jewish and Christian identities; it made sense to me that his spirit would come back here to the home he had loved. A spiritual confidante later told me that Dad had not known who he was. I hope that he will one day, and can find peace.

I am very grateful for the way my life was shaped. My childhood in this most isolated of towns, with its vast spaces and rugged beauty, taught me to be strong, independent and resourceful – or as Pam so characteristically put it, 'You and I may not be academics, Bud, but we grew up streetwise!' This vibrant landscape of contrasts, combined with the cultured lifestyle I enjoyed in New Farm, have woven together to form a unique tapestry of experience that has enriched my life and shaped my destiny.

Acknowledgements

My sincere thanks to Doctor Patricia Gaut of the Willoughby Writers Group, who taught me to develop an appropriate writing style at the beginning of this project, and to Deaconess Doreen Garrick, for transferring my early typewritten sheets onto her computer and for patiently helping me when my son Ian gave me my own word processor.

Special thanks to Barbara Ker Wilson, distinguished editor, author and old friend, who wrote a critical analysis of my first chapters when I asked her if it was worth continuing with my story, and gave positive comments.

Appreciative thanks to my literary agent, Philippa Sandall, for showing the nucleus of the manuscript to my publisher, Bernadette Foley, who was interested and gave it to Amanda O'Connell, eminent consultant editor, to read. I am grateful for Amanda's encouraging criticism and editing. Bernadette has kindly and enthusiastically guided me throughout the writing of the book, and Brianne Tunnicliffe has been an inspirational and supportive editor all the way. These women have become valued friends.

My late husband, John, encouraged and supported me from the project's inception, as he has always done with my writing and with our combined work when we wrote herb and spice books together. He has my thanks and my love forever.

My dear family spurred me on when I gave them my first efforts to read, and I am grateful for their love and enthusiasm. Ian and Elizabeth were readers of the final draft, and I deeply value their comments.